BRITISH LABOUR STRUGGLES:
CONTEMPORARY PAMPHLETS 1727-1850

FRIENDLY SOCIETIES

Seven Pamphlets

1798-1839

Arno Press

A New York Times Company/New York 1972

Reprint Edition 1972 by Arno Press Inc.

Reprinted from copies in the Kress Library
Graduate School of Business Administration,
Harvard University

The imperfections found in this edition
reflect defects in the originals which
could not be eliminated.

BRITISH LABOUR STRUGGLES: CONTEMPORARY PAMPHLETS 1727-1850
ISBN for complete set: 0-405-04410-0

See last pages for complete listing.

Manufactured in the United States of America

Library of Congress Cataloging in Publication Data
Main entry under title:

Friendly societies.

    (British labour struggles:
contemporary pamphlets 1727-1850)
    CONTENTS: The rules and regulations of the Castle
Eden Friendly Society, by M. Scarth [first published
1798].--Rules and regulations to be observed by the
society at Annan [first published 1801].--Articles to be
observed by the members of a friendly society [first published 1807]. [etc.]
    1. Friendly societies--Great Britain. I. Series.
HD7167.F7   334'.7'0942   72-2528
ISBN 0-405-04421-6

Contents

THE

RULES and REGULATIONS

OF THE

Caftle Eden Friendly Society;

WITH

EXTRACTS FROM THE PROCEEDINGS, &c.

TO WHICH ARE ADDED,

EXPLANATORY NOTES and OBSERVATIONS.

By *MICHAEL SCARTH,*

STEWARD OF THAT SOCIETY.

Publifhed at the Requeft of the " Society for bettering the Condition,
and increafing the Comforts of the Poor," with a View
to facilitate fimilar Eftablifhments.

LONDON:

PRINTED FOR W. CLARKE, NEW BOND STREET.

1798.

[Price One Shilling.]

TO THE

PUBLIC.

IN proportion as the eſtabliſhment of Friendly
Societies is extended, it becomes of material con-
ſequence both to the members who compoſe them,
and to the community at large, that they ſhould be
eſtabliſhed upon permanent principles; and, above
all, that the calculations upon which their funds
are grounded ſhould not be fallacious. The diſ-
treſs and diſappointment occaſioned by the bank-
ruptcy of one of theſe Societies are ſenſibly felt both
by the poor and their reſpective pariſhes, through-
out a large diſtrict; whilſt the happy effects of
their permanent proſperity extend themſelves at
leaſt in an equal degree.

It will be obſerved that in theſe Rules, &c. ſome
latitude is taken for the admiſſion of perſons employed in a manufactory. It is earneſtly hoped
that benevolent inſtitutions of this nature may not
be cramped by rules excluding perſons of ſuch
deſcription, ſtill leſs by ſuch rules as unfortu-
nately exiſt in ſome Friendly Societies, for ex-

A 2   cluding

cluding perfons ferving their country in its navy or army, by which thefe eftablifhments become detrimental inftead of ufeful to the general ftate of the nation. As thefe Rules, &c. were drawn by a perfon eminently calculated to form fuch an inftitution, with the affiftance of a gentleman of great refpectability in the profeffion of the law, they will, it is hoped, facilitate any fimilar undertaking.

To make the eftablifhment of Friendly Societies eafy, and to perpetuate their duration and benefits, is the motive of this publication. Happy fhall I be if the benevolent object of the " Society " for bettering the Condition, and increafing the " Comforts of the Poor," fhall be in any fhape forwarded by this communication, in obedience to their requeft.

R. BURDON.

INDEX

INDEX

TO

RULES.

---

(7)

THE

RESOLUTIONS, RULES, ORDERS,

AND

REGULATIONS

FOR THE

GOVERNMENT

OF THE

Caſtle Eden Friendly Society.

WHEREAS by an act of parliament made in Preamble. the thirty-third year of the reign of his Majeſty King George the Third, intituled, " An " Act for the encouragement and relief of Friendly " Societies*," it is enacted—*(here the ſection of*
the

---

* In the latter end of the year 1790, a Friendly Society of three claſſes, was eſtabliſhed at Caſtle Eden. On the Legiſlature recognizing Friendly Societies by paſſing the above act, the Society thought it better to form new Rules, or rather a new Society, than to have the old Rules allowed, they having been found inſufficient for all the purpoſes of the Society; and by admitting the members of the old Society, as is provided by the 32d article of theſe Rules, the funds were transferred, and the old members admitted to the ſame benefits as they were entitled to under the old Rules. By this plan an old Society may be incorporated with a new one, and ſo obtain the benefits of the act of

B   parliament,

the act, which authorizes any number of persons to form Societies, &c. is recited) :

And whereas many persons resident in the parishes of C. E. &c. being convinced of the benefit of such Societies, and having agreed to form themselves into such a Society at C. E. aforesaid, under the name and title of the C. E. Friendly Society, and to become contributors to a fund to be raised and applied to the purposes hereinafter mentioned, did meet at the C. inn, in the parish of **C. E.** aforesaid, on the   day of   in the year   for the purpose of establishing the said Society, and appointing trustees and other officers for transacting and superintending the concerns thereof, and of determining upon and settling rules and regulations for the management and government thereof: At which time and place the following resolutions and rules were proposed and agreed upon, (that is to say :)

Truftees.

2. That R. B. &c. *(here the names of the principal persons within the said parishes, their rectors, curates, and resident magiftrates, are recited)*, shall be, and they are hereby appointed trustees for the funds of the said Society, as hereinafter mentioned.

Stewards.

3. That Mr. M. S. of C. E. shall be, and he is hereby appointed fteward thereof.

Directors.

4. That C. R. &c. *(here the names of twelve of the*

---

parliament, notwithftanding the time being elapfed for the old Societies having their Rules allowed under that act, and confequently there is no neceffity for extending the time for having old Societies allowed, as was done by the 35th Geo. III. c. 3.; and by this method old Societies have a favourable opportunity of revifing their Rules, of which in too many cafes they ftand in great need.

principal

principal yeomen, and the churchwardens of the said parishes, are recited), and all perfons becoming honorary members of this Society, shall be, and they are hereby appointed directors of the said Society, whose office and duty are hereinafter defined *.

5. That notwithstanding the appointment of the aforesaid perfons to be directors, no perfon shall be capable of acting as a director after he shall have been admitted a member of the Society, nor longer than he shall refide in fome one of the aforesaid parishes, excepting honorary members. *Who are capable of acting as directors.*

6. That G. O. &c. *(here the names of twelve fubstantial members of the Society are recited)*, shall be, and they are hereby appointed a committee for *Committee.*

---

* The twelve directors are chofen out of the moft respectable men in the neighbourhood that will take the trouble of acting, and are intended as a check on the committee and members mifapplying the funds. For without a check of this kind, members of Societies are often inclined to divide the money when the Society grows rich. An inftance is ftated by Sir Frederick Eden in his account of Petersfield, vol. ii. p. 223, in which he fays, " There are twelve ale-houfes in this parifh, " but no Friendly Society. Two exifted fome time ago ; but as " foon as the ftock amounted to a few hundreds, the clubs were " diffolved, and the money divided amongft the members ;" and few will be inclined to become benefactors or honorary members, unlefs they have a fecurity for the due and permanent application of their donations. Sir F. in his 1ft vol. p. 603, agrees with the Bath Agricultural Society, that there ought to be a rule in every benefit club, " That no part of their ftock fhall ever be laid out " in the purchafe of lottery tickets, or in any other way which " may rifk any part of their property in games of chance." By having a board of control, and limited as in the 19th and 21ft articles of this Society, the members are prevented from making any fuch mifapplications, or altering the Rules without due confideration.

the

the purpofes hereinafter mentioned, and to continue in office until the firft day of January next, if they fhall fo long live, unlefs they or any of them fhould neglect to qualify as hereafter mentioned, or remove out of the faid parifhes, or be excluded the Society *.

Treafurer.

7. That Mr. G. T. fhall be, and he is hereby appointed treafurer of the Society †.

Clerks.

8. That Mr. T. P. and Mr. W. M. fhall be, and they are hereby appointed clerks of the Society.

Power to difplace treafurer and clerks.

9. That the fteward, directors, and committee, for the time being, fhall have power, from time to time, to difplace and remove the treafurer and clerks for the time being, and to appoint others in the room of fuch of them as fhall be fo removed, or fhall vacate or die.

Firft meeting.

10. That the fteward, directors, committee, treafurer, and clerks, hereby appointed, fhall meet at the houfe of   , or at fome other convenient houfe in the parifh of   , on the fourth Saturday after thefe Rules, Orders, and Regulations fhall be allowed and confirmed by the juftices of the peace, at the general quarter feffions of the peace, or at an adjournment thereof, in and for the county of D. (as directed by the faid act of parliament), between the hours of four and fix o'clock in the afternoon, then and there to qualify as hereinafter mentioned, and to admit as members, the perfons whofe names are hereunto

---

* By an alteration in the 28th article *(fee* page 47) the members are liable to ferve in the committee two years together, it being found better that only fix new ones fhould come in annually.

† In many Societies it would be advifeable to have two treafurers.

subfcribed,

subfcribed, and such other persons as they may
think proper *.

11. That the said treasurer, and all such trea- *Treafurer to
furer or treafurers as shall hereafter be appointed, give security.
before he or they be permitted to take upon him
or them the execution of such office, shall become
bound with two sufficient sureties, for the faithful
execution of such office, and for rendering a true
account of all their receipts, payments, and tranfactions, according to the rules, orders, and regulations of this Society, in such penal sum or sums
of money, as by the steward, directors, and
committee, shall from time to time be thought
expedient; and that all such bond or bonds, to
be given by and on the behalf of such treasurer
or treafurers, shall be given to the clerk of the
peace for the county of   , for the time
being, for the use of this Society †.

12. That

---

* This Society does not limit the number of its members, which is the case with many Societies noted by Sir F.
Eden (vol. ii. p. 23, 566, &c.). Other Societies increase the
terms of admission in proportion to the increase of their funds,
which is proved by Dr. Price to be very imprudent.

† *Form of Bond.* " Know all men by these presents,
" that we, G. T. of C. E. in the county of D. innkeeper [or as
" the case shall be], T. T. of H. in the same county
" and W. L. of C. E. aforesaid   are held and firmly
" bound to G. P. of the city of D. Esq. clerk of the peace for the
" said county of D. in the penal sum of two hundred pounds, of
" good and lawful money of Great Britain, to be paid to the
" said G. P. or his successors, or to his or their certain attorney,
" executors, administrators, or assigns : for which payment to
" be well and truly made, we bind ourselves jointly and seve-
" rally, our respective heirs, executors, and administrators,
" firmly by these presents. Sealed with our seals, dated this
"   day of   in the   year of the reign of our
" Sovereign Lord George the Third, by the grace of God of
" Great

Monthly
meetings.

12. That the steward, directors, committee, treasurer, and clerks, or so many of them as can conveniently attend, shall meet on the fourth Saturday next after the first meeting, between the hours of six and seven o'clock in the evening, at some convenient house in the parish of C. E. to be by them appointed for that purpose, and so shall continue to meet from time to time on every fourth Saturday from the time of such meeting, to

---

" Great Britain, France, and Ireland, king, defender of the
" faith, and so forth, and in the year of our Lord
    " Whereas the above-bounden G. T. hath been duly elected
" and appointed treasurer of and for the Society called the C. E.
" F. Society, in the said county, lately established, under the
" authority of an act of parliament passed in the thirty-third year
" of the reign of his present Majesty, intituled, ' An Act for the
" encouragement and relief of Friendly Societies :' The condi-
" tion therefore of the above-written obligation is such, that if
" the said G. T. his executors and administrators, do and shall
" from time to time, and at all times hereafter, upon demand,
" made in pursuance of any order by the said Society, or any
" committee appointed by them for that purpose, render a just
" and true account of all his receipts, payments, and transac-
" tions relative to the said Society, and from time to time, on
" the like demand, pay over all the monies remaining in his or
" their hands or custody, to any future treasurer or treasurers to
" be appointed by the said Society, or to such other person or
" persons as such Society shall appoint; and if the said G. T.
" shall and do from time to time, and at all times hereafter, in
" all other respects well and faithfully execute the office of trea-
" surer of and for the said Society, pursuant to the rules, or-
" ders, and regulations thereof for the time being, and in all
" matters lawful pay obedience to the same, then the above-
" written obligation shall be void, otherwise the same shall be
" and remain in full force and virtue.
    " Signed, sealed, and delivered, in the presence of us,
            " R. W.   " G. T. (P. S.)
            " J. A.   " T. T. (P. S.)
                                    " W. L. (P. S.)"
                                            receive

receive the monthly and other payments and contributions, to admit new members, and tranſact the other buſineſs of the Society. At which meetings the members' names ſhall be called over as they ſtand in the entry-book ; and each member's contributions and fines ſhall be paid to the treaſurer, or his deputy, at the time ſuch member's name ſhall be called ; and if not then paid *, ſuch member ſhall incur the penalty or forfeiture hereinafter mentioned. After all the members' names ſhall have been called over, if any member have any perſon to propoſe as a new member, or any matter to ſubmit to the conſideration of the Society, he ſhall ſtand up and addreſs himſelf to the ſteward, and immediately after having ſpoken, ſhall ſit down in his place ; and any other member who ſhall wiſh to ſpeak on the ſubject, ſhall, in like manner, deliver his ſentiments in his turn ; after which the ſteward ſhall put the matter to vote, and if ſeven of the committee ſhall vote in favour of the propoſition, the ſame being then approved of by the ſteward, and three or more of the directors preſent, the perſon propoſed ſhall be elected a member, or the matter propoſed ſhall become binding to the Society as the act of the meeting ; and as well in the election of members, as upon all other occaſions, ſeven balls of the committee, with the ſubſequent conſent of the ſteward, and three of the directors at the leaſt, ſhall be taken and deemed to be the act of the Society at large, and be binding upon every member thereof ; and

---

* To give abſent members more time, and prevent fines, it is uſual in this Society to call the names of abſentees a ſecond and third time after the contributions of the members preſent have been received.

all

all refolutions of the Society fhall be entered in
the order-book, and be figned by the fteward,
three of the directors, and feven of the committee,
at the leaft; but nothing which fhall alter, vacate, or refcind any of thefe refolutions, fhall be
refolved or agreed upon at any monthly meeting,
but only at the annual meeting. And fo foon as
all the bufinefs of each monthly meeting fhall be
finifhed, the books fhall be clofed and locked up
in a cheft to be provided for that purpofe, which
fhall not be opened again till the next monthly
meeting. After all the bufinefs fhall be done,
and the cheft locked (but not before on any pretence whatfoever), there fhall be expended in
liquor out of the fund, five fhillings, and no
more *. Whenever the fteward cannot attend

* When meetings are held at inns or public houfes, it
is better to allow a fmall fixed fum to be expended for liquor out
of the general fund at each meeting, than that the members
fhould contribute individually; for it appears to be the cafe in
fome Societies mentioned by Sir F. Eden and others, that
the fum expended is equal to one-fixth and one-fourth,
and in fome inftances one-third of the money paid into the
fund. There is great reafon to believe that many Societies
have been eftablifhed more for the advantage of the innkeepers
than of the members. If the expending fuch a fum fhould not
be thought a fufficient recompence for fire, candles, &c. an annual fum may be allowed for that purpofe. This Society allowed
at the end of laft year one guinea, which with five fhillings fpent
monthly, was confidered a fufficient recompence; and it very
feldom happened that the committee or members fpent any thing
at the meetings, the five fhillings worth of ale being found fufficient, as no drink is allowed till after all the bufinefs is done,
and the members are obliged, under a penalty, to quit the houfe
at ten o'clock; the bufinefs alfo being done by a committee, &c.
a great part of the members pay their money in advance, or fend
it by others.

the

the meetings, he fhall fend his key to one of the
clerks, who fhall officiate in his ftead.

13. That no perfon fhall be capable of acting
as fteward, or director, or as one of the committee, until he fhall make and fign a declaration, that he will in all things faithfully execute
the feveral trufts and powers committed to him by
the Rules, Orders, and Regulations of this Society * ; neither fhall any perfon be capable of
acting as fteward, unlefs he be a member of this
Society, and refide in the parifh of C. E.

*Steward.
Who is ca-
pable of act-
ing as fuch.*

14. That in cafe the fteward for the time being,
or any of the directors or committee, fhall die,
refufe to act, or vacate their offices by removing
out of the faid parifhes, or otherwife, then and in
every fuch cafe, the furvivors of the fteward, directors, and committee, as the cafe fhall be, fhall,
at the next monthly meeting of this Society, after
fuch death, refufal to act, vacating the office, or
otherwife, appoint a general meeting of the members to be holden at the then next monthly meeting, for the purpofe of appointing others to fill fuch

*Appoint-
ment of
fteward, di-
rectors, and
committee.*

---

* The declarations are printed in a book, and are to the following effect : " I B. C. of D. in the parifh of
" do hereby moft folemnly promife and declare, that I will in
" all things well and faithfully execute the feveral trufts and
" powers committed to me, as   of the C. E. Friendly
" Society, by the Refolutions, Rules, Orders, and Regulations
" of that Society, according to the true intent and meaning
" thereof ; and that I will not, at any time or times hereafter,
" give my confent to any new Refolution, Rule, Order, or Re-
" gulation, to alter the whole, or any part or parts of the pre-
" fent Refolutions, Rules, Orders, or Regulations, unlefs I
" fhall believe fuch alteration, or alterations, to be for the benefit
" of the whole of the members of the faid Society.
                                                                " B. C."
   " The above declaration was made and figned by the faid
" B. C. the   day of   in the prefence of

C   vacan-

vacancies, and fo from time to time upon every fubfequent vacancy. And if any office be vacated after the firft day of November in any year, then and in fuch cafe, the appointment fhall be referred to the next yearly meeting. At all elections, the fteward and committee fhall be entitled to vote as members of this Society, and in cafe of an equality of votes, the fteward fhall have and exercife a cafting vote.

Monthly contributions. 15. That the funds of this Society fhall be in the nature of fhares amongft its members for the time being, and the fums to be contributed and paid by each member, for or in refpect of each fingle fhare in the faid Society, fhall be after the following rate, (that is to fay :)

If the member be under 22 years of age, *s.* *d.*

		s.	*d.*
when admitted, he fhall pay per month		1	0
If above 22, and under 23 years		1	0½
If above 23, and under 24 years		1	1
If above 24, and under 25 years		1	1½
If above 25, and under 26 years		1	2
If above 26, and under 27 years		1	2½
If above 27, and under 28 years		1	3
If above 28, and under 29 years		1	3½
If above 29, and under 30 years		1	4
If above 30, and under 31 years		1	4½
If above 31, and under 32 years		1	5
If above 32, and under 33 years		1	5½
If above 33, and under 34 years		1	6
If above 34, and under 35 years		1	6½
If above 35, and under 36 years		1	7
If above 36, and under 37 years		1	7½
If above 37, and under 38 years		1	8
If above 38, and under 39 years		1	8½
If above 39, and under 40 years		1	9
If above 40, and under 41 years		1	9½
If above 41, and under 42 years		1	10
If above 42, and under 43 years		1	10½

If

	s.	d.

If above 43, and under 44 years, per mon. 1 11
If above 44, and under 45 years   1 11½
If above 44, and under 46 years   2 0

But each member, under the age of forty-five, may take and pay for as many ſhares as he pleaſes, and ſhall be entitled to a proportionate relief, as hereinafter mentioned *.

16. That if any perſon above the age of twenty-two years, who ſhall be admitted a member of this Society, ſhall be deſirous of being put upon the ſame footing in point of monthly contribution, as if he had been admitted a member under that age, he ſhall only contribute the ſum of one ſhilling per month, during his life, if ſuch perſon do pay, on admiſſion, or at the next monthly meeting afterwards, a groſs ſum according to his age, as ſpecified in the ſcheme or table following, for each ſhare that he may chooſe to take, (that is to ſay :) Contributions on admiſſion.

---

* This and the compoſition table in the next article are formed from Dr. Price's computations, which were made at the requeſt of the committee of the Houſe of Commons. See App. 1. Rev. Payments, vol. ii. p. 409—430. Though theſe are more in favour of the old than young members, it being neceſſary to keep the payments for old men as low as poſſible, to induce them to enter for if they were to contribute according to Dr. Price's tables, very few would become members). yet, upon the whole, the funds are not injured, but rather increaſed, there being more young men admitted than old The compoſition tables for old ages is much lower than Dr. Price's, notwithſtanding which, very few have availed themſelves of the advantage. The ob-ject in framing the Caſtle Eden tables, was to make the monthly contributions fully equal to the diſburſements, and to induce per-ſons of all ages, under forty-ſix, to become members, without calculating exactly what each ought to pay. The funds being in the nature of ſhares, each member has an opportunity of con-tributing according to his or her ability or inclination ; and in many inſtances a married man contributes for two ſhares, one ſhare for himſelf, and one for his wife.

If

	£.	s.	d.
If such member be above 22, and under 23 years of age, when admitted	0	5	0
If above 23, and under 24 years	0	10	0
If above 24, and under 25 years	0	15	0
If above 25, and under 26 years	1	0	0
If above 26, and under 27 years	1	5	0
If above 27, and under 28 years	1	10	0
If above 28, and under 29 years	1	15	0
If above 29, and under 30 years	2	0	0
If above 30, and under 31 years	2	6	0
If above 31, and under 32 years	2	12	0
If above 32, and under 33 years	2	18	0
If above 33, and under 34 years	3	4	0
If above 34, and under 35 years	3	10	0
If above 35, and under 36 years	3	18	0
If above 36, and under 37 years	4	6	0
If above 37, and under 38 years	4	14	0
If above 38, and under 39 years	5	2	0
If above 39, and under 40 years	5	10	0
If above 40, and under 41 years	6	0	0
If above 41, and under 42 years	6	10	0
If above 42, and under 43 years	7	0	0
If above 43, and under 44 years	7	10	0
If above 44, and under 45 years	8	0	0
If above 45, and under 46 years	8	10	0

Funeral expenses, how made up to the fund.

17. That in order to keep up the general fund, each member shall pay six-pence for each share, and three-pence for each half share, to which he may be a contributor, on the decease of every member for whose funeral this Society shall have any disbursements to make. Such contribution to be paid at the first monthly meeting after the disbursement *.   18. That

---

* By this plan, the disbursements at the death of the members affect the funds of the Society only in proportion to the number of its members. When it shall consist of two hundred shares, the fund will remain untouched. It would be a more certain

18. That the monthly contribution of each **Times of** member fhall commence and be made on the firft **payment.** monthly meeting after his or her admiffion, and fhall continue to be made during his or her life, at the monthly meetings to be holden on every fourth Saturday; but that any member may make payments in advance for three months, or any other length of time *, if he or fhe think proper; and in cafe any member fhall die before the expiration of the term for which fuch payments in advance fhall have been made, a proportionable part thereof fhall be refunded to his widow; and if no widow, to his legal reprefentatives.

19. That the monthly contributions, fines, and **Society's ef-** all other fums that may be received on account of **fects, how to be fecured.** this Society, fhall be put into a cheft (to be kept by the treafurer), which fhall have three good locks, with a different key to each; one of which keys fhall be kept by the fteward, another by one of the committee, to be named for that purpofe by the directors (and in cafe he cannot attend, he may fend fuch key with any other of the committee), and the third key by the treafurer; and fo foon as the fund fhall amount to twenty pounds, ten pounds (part thereof) fhall be invefted in the public funds †; or placed out at intereft

upon

---

certain way of protecting the fund, if the money paid at the death of the members was proportioned to the number of exifting fhares.

* The allowing payments in advance, is convenient to members living at a diftance from the place where the Society meets.

† It is abfolutely neceffary to be very careful in putting out the money as fpeedily as poffible, in order to get the advantage of intereft; for without this, all, or the greateft part of Friendly Societies will not be able to diftribute the benefits they propofe.

upon real or perfonal fecurity, to be approved of by the fteward, directors, and committee, by fome writing under their hands.

20. That when any money fhall be invefted, or placed out at intereft, on account of this Society, the ftock fhall be purchafed, and the fecurity made or taken in the name of the truftees for the time being, or fuch three of them, as the fteward, directors, and committee, fhall appoint, in truft for the general ufes of this Society; and the

---

propofe. If the great accumulation of compound intereft were better underftood, it is reafonable to fuppofe that thofe who have the management of the funds belonging to Friendly Societies would attend to this more than they do. It will furprife them to be told, that five hundred pounds, at five per cent. compound intereft, will amount to above fixty-four thoufand pounds within a century, and to upwards of *a million* within one hundred and fixty years. The many loffes which Friendly Societies have fuftained, make the members very diffident in lending any part of their funds. Sir F. Eden, in his " State of the Poor," vol. ii. p. 34, fays, that feveral Societies at Chefter broke up in confequence of lofing their funds, partly by the failure of a bank, and partly by an unfuccefsful canal near that city; and in the 3d vol. p. 712, that a Society at Efher, Surrey, was diffolved in confequence of having loft three hundred pounds by the failure of fome tradef-men, on which the members divided the remainder; and in p. 889, he fays, that three or four Societies have been diffolved in the neighbourhood of Llanferras, Denbighfhire, owing to their being defrauded of a great part of their funds. If the Le-giflature were to encourage Friendly Societies, *eftablifhed under fpecific rules,* to lay out part of their funds in the purchafe of go-vernment fecurities, by exempting their powers of attorney from ftamp duty, poftage, &c. it is probable that fuch Societies would become more general, and great benefit would arife to the nation at large. An office might be eftablifhed in London under the authority of parliament, for the benefit of Friendly Societies, and their ftock concerns managed by an accountant-general. The money might with great eafe be paid and received through the collectors of excife.

truftees

truftees fhall from time to time, when requefted, execute powers of attorney for receiving the dividends and intereft, as the fame fhall become due half-yearly; and alfo for receiving or recovering the principal money to be invefted or placed out, or any part thereof, to fuch perfon or perfons only as the fteward, directors, and committee, for the time being, fhall by writing under their hands direct. But the truftees, fteward, directors, committee, treafurers, and clerks, refpectively, fhall not be anfwerable nor accountable for involuntary loffes, nor one for the other, nor for the acts or defaults of each other, but each perfon for himfelf alone.

21. That all reafonable expenfes of the truftees, *Officers to be reimburfed expenfes.* fteward, directors, treafurers, and clerks, in the execution of their feveral offices, fhall be paid out of the funds of this Society; and that they fhall refpectively be indemnified out of the faid funds againft all actions, fuits, damages, and expenfes whatfoever, which may be brought againft or fuftained by them, or any of them, on account of their, or any of their acting in and executing the powers and trufts hereby repofed in them (excepting that the truftees and directors fhall defray their own expenfes at all yearly meetings); and no money fhall be taken out of the *No money to be paid without an order in writing.* cheft on any pretence whatever, without a previous order in writing figned by the fteward, three of the directors, and feven of the committee at the leaft; and the treafurer fhall be anfwerable for, and make good, all the money which he fhall from time to time receive on account of this Society, excepting that for which he can produce fuch orders, and excepting the weekly allowance to members in ficknefs; in which latter cafe an order in writing from the fteward alone fhall be fufficient.

22. That

Admitting members.

22. That after the firſt meeting, no perſon ſhall be admitted a member, unleſs propoſed by a member of this Society, at a monthly or yearly meeting ; and at the time of propoſing a new member, two ſhillings and ſixpence ſhall be paid to the treaſurer for the uſe of the general fund : and in order that in the interval proper inquiry may be made into his character, the perſon propoſed ſhall be ballotted for by the committee at the then next monthly or yearly meeting (excepting women, who may be admitted at the ſame monthly or yearly meeting at which they may be propoſed, with the conſent of the ſteward, three of the directors, and ſeven of the committee, they being, by the 34th article, exempted from receiving weekly allowances in caſes of ſickneſs or infirmity) ; and if on ſuch ballot there ſhall appear ſeven balls for him, he ſhall be admitted a member, provided the ſteward and three of the directors, at the leaſt, conſent to his admiſſion, but not otherwiſe ; and if the perſon propoſed ſhall be rejected, the two ſhillings and ſixpence paid to the treaſurer ſhall be returned.

Age and declaration.

23. That no perſon ſhall be admitted a member of this Society under the age of ten years *, or above the age of forty-ſix years † ; and the

---

* Ten years was the age fixed on account of a manufactory (ſee Art. 23) ; but the writer is of opinion that none ought to be admitted under eighteen years of age, unleſs under particular circumſtances.

† This Society admits to a greater age than moſt Societies, which it is enabled to do by the contributions being in proportion to the age when the member is admitted. Many of the Societies mentioned by Sir F. Eden, appear to limit the ages of admiſſion ſo as to prevent many eligible perſons from being admitted, particularly one reſpectfully mentioned at Epſom, vol. iii. p. 697, in which the higheſt age is twenty-five years.

perſon

perfon fo admitted (or fome member for him or her) fhall, at the time of his or her admiffion, make and fign a declaration, in the prefence of the fteward, or three or more directors, to the following effect, (that is to fay:)

" I, A. B. of C. D in the parifh of E. and county of D. (labourer, or as the cafe may be), of the age of   years, in the month of   laft, to the beft of my knowledge and belief, do requeft to be admitted a member of the C E. Friendly Society, and to become entitled to the benefit to arife from fhare, for which I bind myfelf to pay to the treafurer, at the firft monthly meeting after my admiffion, the fum of and on every fourth Saturday afterwards (fo long as I continue a member)   fhilling   ; and fuch other contributions as may become due: and I do hereby folemnly promife and declare, that if I am admitted a member, I will in all things well and truly fulfil, keep, and obferve, the rules, orders, and regulations of the Society, and to the utmoft of my power promote its interefts.

" Witnefs my hand this   day of in the year of our Lord one thoufand hundred   " *

---

* The declarations as above, are printed and bound in a book, with a memorandum of admiffion at the bottom of each, to the following effect : " Be it remembered, that the above-
" named A. B. was this   day of   in the year of
" our Lord   duly admitted a member into the Caftle
" Eden Friendly Society, and entered in the books kept for that
" purpofe ; and that if he in every refpect conform to the refo-
" lutions, rules, orders, and regulations of that Society, he
" will be entitled to the benefits thereof.
                                   " M. S. Steward.
                                   " W. M. Clerk."
            D   24. That

Capital to belong to the Society. 24. That the capital ftock to arife from the fines, and monthly and other contributions, and the dividends, intereft, and yearly produce thereof, fhall be the property of the members of the C. E. Benefits in ficknefs. Friendly Society for the time being; and every member of the Society, who fhall duly conform to the rules, orders, and regulations thereof, fhall, for each fhare which he fhall have in the fund, be entitled to relief in cafes of ficknefs or infirmity as hereinafter mentioned, and fo in proportion for half a fhare, (that is to fay :) To fix fhillings a week when confined in bed, or to his bedchamber, by ficknefs, lamenefs, or infirmity, and unable to go out of the houfe, or perform any kind of work, until he fhall be able to walk out, or to labour in any degree, and then to three fhillings a week, when fo able to walk or labour; but both thefe allowances to ceafe, when fuch member fhall be able to follow his ufual occupation, or to earn three fhillings a week; fuch of thefe fums as fhall be due to be regularly paid, provided the fame be requefted, from the firft Saturday after the member's illnefs fhall be certified to the fteward *. Sums to be paid at a member's death. And the fum of five pounds for each fhare, and fifty fhillings for each half-fhare, fhall be paid at the death of each member to his widow, or if no widow, to any perfon appointed, in writing, by him to receive the fame, and if no fuch perfon be appointed, then to his legal reprefentatives: but the fteward, directors, and committee, fhall have an election, either to pay the money to the perfons laft men-

---

* The allowance in ficknefs is about one-third higher than Dr. Price's; but members receiving in ficknefs are debarred from annuities for the fame fhares, and on that account this allowance in ficknefs may be afforded.

tioned,

tioned, or to expend two guineas, part of fuch
allowance, in any manner they may think proper,
in the funeral of fuch deceafed member, the remainder to be applied in the following manner,
(that is to fay:) If the deceafed member fhall
have left any child or children under the age of
twelve years, in that cafe, the fame fhall be applied for fuch child or children's benefit, in fuch
manner as the fteward, directors, and committee
fhall think proper; and if there be no child or
children under that age, then to be paid to the
widow, if any; and if no widow, to the perfon
appointed in writing, as aforefaid; and if no fuch
perfon, then to the legal reprefentatives of the
deceafed member. And the widow of each member of this Society, who fhall die after having
contributed to the fund during fifteen years, for
any number of fhares or half-fhares, without
having received an annuity as hereafter mentioned, or any other relief from this Society, for
fuch fhares or half-fhares, after he attained the
age of twenty-one years, to whom he fhall have
been married one year, fhall be entitled to claim
and receive, during the time fhe may continue
his widow, a clear annuity of four pounds a year
for each fhare, on account of which he fhall not
have received relief, and two pounds a year for
each fuch half-fhare, by quarterly payments, viz.
on the laft monthly meeting in March, June,
September, and December; the firft payment of
fuch annuity to commence and be made on the
firft of thefe monthly meetings which fhall happen next after fuch member's death; and in cafe
fuch member fhall die without leaving a widow,
but leaving an orphan child or children under the
age of twelve years, the like annuity fhall, at
fuch times, be applied for fuch child or children's
benefit, in fuch manner as the fteward, directors,
and committee, for the time being, fhall think

proper,

proper, until the youngeft of fuch children fhall attain the age of twelve years *. And each woman being a member of this Society, after having contributed to the fund for fifteen years, fhall be entitled to claim and receive an annuity of four pounds a year for each fhare, and two pounds for each half-fhare, after attaining the age of fifty years, and until fhe attain the age of fixty years, to be paid in manner mentioned in the twenty-fifth article for the payment of annuities to commence at fixty years of age †

Annuities. 25. That the members of this Society, of or above fixty years of age, who in ficknefs or infirmity fhall prefer an annuity to weekly payments, fhall be entitled to claim and receive progreffive annuities as follows : viz.

Each member of the age of fixty years, and under feventy years, an annuity of fix pounds;

The fame, or any other member, when of the age of feventy, and under eighty years, an annuity of eight pounds ;

The fame, or any other member, when of the age of eighty years, and under ninety years, an annuity of ten pounds ;

The fame, or any other member, when of the age of ninety years or upwards, an annuity of twelve pounds ;

---

* The allowing widows or orphans an annuity of four pounds per annum, on each fhare on which the member fhall have received no benefit after fubfcribing for fifteen years, is a great inducement for not claiming when in ficknefs, and thereby enables the fund to make good the payments.

† Women are allowed to receive an annuity ten years fooner than men, in confequence of their not receiving in ficknefs, and of the whole of their contributions being funk at their death, without the payment of any annuities to their widowers or orphan children. If they were not to receive an annuity until fixty years of age, fewer men would contribute for their wives.

during their refpective natural lives *. Such
annuities to commence and be computed from
the firft day of January after each fuch member fhall have attained the age of fixty, feventy, eighty, or ninety years refpectively, according to their refpective declarations, delivered
at

---

* In order to fhow the advantage of annuities, this Society has thought it advifeable to publifh a table (as below) to
fhow the amount of what may be received for one fhare from
fifty to ninety-fix years of age, and alfo to prove the neceffity of
forming a confiderable fund.

TABLE, *fhowing the Amount of an Annuity payable for one Share in
the C. E. Friendly Society.*

	To a Man. £.	To a Woman. £.
If the member live to 51 years of age, the Society will have paid by quarterly payments	—	4
to 52 years	—	8
to 53 years	—	12
to 54 years	—	16
to 55 years	—	20
to 56 years	—	24
to 57 years	—	28
to 58 years	—	32
to 59 years	—	36
to 60 years	—	40
to 61 years	6	46
to 62 years	12	52
to 63 years	18	58
to 64 years	24	64
to 65 years	30	70
to 66 years	36	76
to 67 years	42	82
to 68 years	48	88
to 69 years	54	94
to 70 years	60	100
to 71 years	68	108
to 72 years	76	116

at the time of their admiffion into the Society: the faid annuities to be paid by monthly payments at each monthly meeting *, for each fhare, and

	To a Man. £.	To a Woman. £.
If the member live to 73 years of age, the Society will have paid by quarterly payments	84	124
to 74 years	92	132
to 75 years	100	140
to 76 years	108	148
to 77 years	116	156
to 78 years	124	164
to 79 years	132	172
to 80 years	140	180
to 81 years	150	190
to 82 years	160	200
to 83 years	170	210
to 84 years	180	220
to 85 years	190	230
to 86 years	200	240
to 87 years	210	250
to 88 years	220	260
to 89 years	230	270
to 90 years	240	280
to 91 years	252	292
to 92 years	264	304
to 93 years	276	316
to 94 years	288	328
to 95 years	300	340

And fo on, at the rate of 12l. a year during life.

A member may contribute for any number of fhares or half-fhares; but no annuity is payable until the member have contributed fifteen years; nor for any fhare on which relief in ficknefs has been received.

* It was thought better to have the payments of the annuities quarterly, to fave abfent members the trouble of procuring monthly certificates of their being alive, &c.

Many Societies exclude their members upon a change of their employment to a more hazardous one, fuch as the army, fea-fervice.

and fo in proportion for each half-fhare, for which
fuch member may then contribute, and for which
he has received no relief in cafes of ficknefs,
lamenefs, or infirmity. But no fuch annuity
fhall be payable in any cafe for any fhare, where
a member has before received relief in any other
mode from the fund of this Society.

26. That no member fhall be entitled to relief Exceptions.
from this Society until he fhall have been a member for one year; nor to any allowance in ficknefs
after he fhall have become entitled to, and been
elected to receive an annuity; nor to any allowance for any difeafe, diftemper, or infirmity, he
may have had when he was admitted a member;
nor for any diftemper contracted by lewdnefs; nor
for any lamenefs, misfortune, or accident, that
fhall have happened to him by quarrelling,
drunkennefs, or gaming; nor fhall any member
be entitled to relief who fhall refufe to have his
diforder examined by any phyfician, furgeon, or
apothecary, appointed by this Society; nor if
charged with any treafonable or felonious matter,
until he fhall be legally acquitted of the fame.
But if any member fhall die before he has been a
member for twelve months, the full amount of
what he may have contributed or paid to the fund
of the Society fhall be returned to his widow, or
if no widow, to any perfon appointed by him in
writing to receive the fame, or if no fuch perfon,
to his legal reprefentatives.

27. That to the intent every member may have Vifitors.

---

fervice, mines, &c. In Societies where the members have an
option between taking relief during ficknefs, or an annuity in old
age, it feems reafonable to allow perfons fo changing their employment to continue members, guarding, perhaps, againft their
receiving relief for any lamenefs, misfortune, difeafe, diftemper,
or infirmity, which might happen to them in confequence of following a more dangerous profeffion than that they were employed
in when admitted members.

relief

relief when entitled thereto, fix refpectable members fhall, at every yearly meeting, be elected vifitors, viz. two for the parifh of C. E. two for the parifh of M. and two for the parifh of E.; whofe duty it fhall be to attend the fick members in their refpective parifhes on receiving notice for that purpofe, and to certify their condition weekly to the fteward; alfo to carry or convey to the fick or other members their allowances, which fhall be paid to the proper hands of each member, and not otherwife; and if the fick member fhall not be capable of applying his allowance properly, the vifitors fhall fee the fame laid out

Certificates from diftant members. or applied for his benefit. But if any member, who fhall be entitled to relief, fhall not refide within any of the aforefaid parifhes, in that cafe, upon the fteward's being properly certified by writing under the hand or hands of the phyfician, furgeon, minifter, churchwardens, or overfeers of the parifh or place wherein the member may be or refide, or any three of them, that fuch member is entitled to receive relief, the fame fhall be paid to the bearer of the certificate *. No

member

---

* Forms or blank certificates of members being fick, are delivered to them when admitted, or on application for the fame, at the bottom of which is a note how it is to be filled up and fent, of which the following is a copy: " This is to cer-
" tify that   of
" a member of the Caftle Eden Friendly Society,
"
"
" and is unable to
" or
" Witnefs   hand this   day of   179

" ☞ The above certificate muft be filled up according to the
" circumftances of the member's cafe. If he wifh to claim
" the

member ſhall be obliged to ſerve as a viſitor for
more than one year together.

28. That every member of this Society who Forfeits,
ſhall neglect to pay, or to cauſe to be paid, his
monthly and other contributions, ſhall, for the
firſt month for which he ſhall be in arrear, forfeit
the ſum of three-pence, and for the ſecond month
the ſum of ſix-pence; and if the ſame be in arrear at the third monthly meeting, ſuch member
ſhall be expelled the Society: and every member
who ſhall be drunk, or in any manner diſordered
with liquor, during the time he ſhall be receiving
relief in lameneſs, ſickneſs, or infirmity, from this
Society, ſhall for every ſuch offence forfeit five
ſhillings; and if any member ſhall be drunk at a
monthly meeting, or ſhall quarrel with any other
member, or propoſe any kind of play or gaming,
or offer to lay any wager, or profanely curſe or

" the half-allowance, the words ' follow his uſual occupation,'
" or ' earn three ſhillings a week,' muſt be added: but if his
" caſe require the full allowance, ' to go out of the houſe,' or
" ' to perform any kind of work,' muſt be written in the blank
" ſpaces left for that purpoſe. And the certificate muſt be
" ſigned by the phyſician, ſurgeon, miniſter, churchwardens,
" or overſeers of the pariſh or place wherein the member may
" be when ſick, and ſent to the ſteward of the Society, who
" will order the money due for relief to be paid to the bearer
" (therefore the member muſt be cautious by whom he may ſend
" his certificate)."

To ſave trouble, on the back thereof are printed a blank order
for payment, and receipt, to the following effect: " To the
" Treaſurer of the Caſtle Eden Friendly Society—Pay unto
" the within named   ſhillings and
" pence, for   weeks ſickneſs,   day of
"   179
"   Steward.
" Received   day of   179   of the
" treaſurer of the Caſtle Eden Friendly Society the above-men-
" tioned ſum of   ſhillings and   pence."

E   ſwear,

fwear, or call or addrefs a member by any other
than his proper name, or fhall ftay at the houfe
where the Society fhall meet later than ten
o'clock at night, except he be detained by bufinefs
of the Society, he fhall forfeit for each fuch
offence one fhilling; and if any member fhall
not obferve the rules which the fteward fhall from
time to time make for regulating the monthly or
other meetings, he fhall for each offence forfeit
three-pence; and each member who fhall be appointed a vifitor, and fhall not difcharge his duty
to the fatisfaction of the fteward, directors, and
committee, fhall for every neglect forfeit two
fhillings and fixpence; and each member who
fhall not appear, and anfwer to his name when
called on at the yearly meeting, and then pay
to the treafurer one fhilling for dinner and liquor,
fhall forfeit one fhilling (except perfons under
twenty-one years of age); and each member who
fhall be appointed of the committee, and fhall
neglect to attend the monthly meetings, except
prevented by ficknefs, or other fufficient caufe to
be allowed by the fteward, directors, and committee, fhall for each neglect forfeit fix-pence;
but no member fhall be obliged to ferve in
fuch committee two years together * ; and if
any perfon, having the cuftody of a key, neglect
to carry or fend the fame as herein before directed,
to the houfe where the monthly meetings are held,
before feven o'clock of the evening of the day
when the fame fhall be held, he fhall forfeit for
each neglect one fhilling; and if any member,
at any meeting of this Society, fhall enter into
any political or religious difpute, or introduce any

---

* Altered. *(See* p. 47.)

difloyal

difloyal or feditious fong or toaft, he fhall for
each offence forfeit fixpence *.

29. That any member who fhall not pay his Payment of
forfeits when demanded, or at the next monthly forfeits.
meeting, fhall incur fuch further forfeitures or
expulfion, in the fame manner as if his monthly
contributions were in arrear.

30. That any member who fhall take any ad- Offences
vantage of this Society, by diffembling any fick- which fub-
nefs or infirmity, or fhall give in a falfe account members to
of his age, or ufe any kind of fraud towards the exclufion.
Society, or fhall neglect to pay, or to caufe to be
paid, his monthly or other payments for three
months after the fame fhall be due, and fhall not
pay them on or before the third monthly meeting
immediately after fuch offence has been committed, he fhall for any fuch offence or neglect be
expelled from this Society, and have no title or
claim to any part of the funds thereof. But any Difputes to
member who may be fined or expelled, or fhall be fettled by
think himfelf aggrieved by any act, matter, or arbitration.
thing, done, or omitted to be done, by this Society, fhall, at a monthly or yearly meeting, deliver to the fteward in writing under his hand a
ftatement of his grievance, and requeft that the
fame may be referred to arbitration, and fhall
name in fuch ftatement a refpectable perfon refiding within any one of the aforefaid parifhes,
but not a member of the Society, as a referee on
his part; and at the fame, or at the following
monthly meeting, the fteward, directors, and
committee, fhall nominate and appoint another
refpectable perfon refiding within one of the faid

---

* In drawing thefe Rules, it was thought right to have no
fines but fuch as fhould be connected with the well-being of
the Society, leaving the laws of the country to operate in all cafes
againft which they have provided.

three

three parifhes, but not a member, as a referee on the part of this Society; which two perfons fhall with all convenient fpeed meet and appoint a third perfon, not being a member, to act with them; which three perfons, or any two of them, fhall have liberty to infpect the rules, orders, and regulations of this Society, and all books and papers belonging thereto; and after fully examining the matter of fuch complaint, they, or any two of them, fhall make fuch award, order, or determination, in writing, as to them fhall feem juft; and fuch award, order, or determination, fhall be binding and conclufive on all the parties, and fhall be final to all intents and purpofes. But if the Society neglect or refufe to appoint fuch referee, or if the referees neglect or refufe to make an award for forty days after they are appointed, then, and in fuch cafe, the complaint fhall be determined by two or more juftices of the peace, in manner directed by the faid act of parliament.

How the members of the old Society may be admitted.

31. That if the members of the firft and fecond claffes of the old C. E. Friendly Society refolve to incorporate themfelves with this Society, and to transfer all their ftock and funds into the ftock and funds thereof, they fhall be admitted into this Society, without refpect being had to their ages, on contributing after the fame rate as they now contribute to their prefent Society, and fhall become entitled to the following benefits and advantages, (that is to fay:) the members of the firft clafs to the fame benefits as if they had refpectively contributed according to the rates herein before fpecified; and the members of the fecond clafs to the fame benefits as if they had refpectively contributed for half a fhare according to the rate herein before fpecified, and fhall be entitled to allowances in ficknefs or infirmity as if they had continued in their old Society; but

no

no fuch member fhall become entitled to receive
any annuity till he fhall have contributed for fifteen years to the funds of this Society, and then
only to the fame annuity as if he were of the
age of fixty years, and to increafe every ten years
in the manner herein before fpecified.

32. That any perfon under the age of forty-five
years fhall be permitted to contribute for any
number of fhares, or half-fhares, in this Society,
and be entitled to a proportionate benefit therefrom ; and may increafe his original fhare, or
fhares, at any time or times after his admiffion, on
contributing according to his age at the time he
fhall make fuch increafe. No member fhall be
entitled to receive more than fix fhillings a week
in cafes of ficknefs or infirmity, but he fhall be
entitled to the fame annuity and benefit for each
additional fhare, or half-fhare, more than one, as
if he had received no relief or benefit from the
Society ; and for the one fhare on which he may
have received any relief in ficknefs or infirmity,
he fhall be entitled to the fame benefit as if he
had no other fhare or fhares. *Perfons may contribute for any number of fhares or half-fhares.*

33. That notwithftanding any thing herein-
before contained, if Meff. S. manufacturers at
C. E. aforefaid, will enter all perfons * above
ten, and under forty-five years of age, that are
now ferving, or may hereafter ferve under them, *How perfons employed in a manufactory are to be admitted.*

* Where manufacturers, &c. agree to enter *all* their apprentices, journeymen, &c. it may be thought reafonable to
admit all without exception ; but then particular care fhould be
taken to provide, that none fhould be entitled to relief for any
complaint they may have had when they were entered, as is the
cafe in this Society. *(See Art.* 26.) And Societies will no doubt
take into their confideration the healthfulnefs, &c. of the employment, before they agree to fo general an admiffion. With refpect
to the age, *fee* p. 24.

in the parifh of C. E. aforefaid; and who, by
fuch fervice, may gain fettlements in that parifh,
into this Society, and continue to pay, or to caufe
to be paid, the monthly and other contributions
herein before mentioned for all fuch perfons, fo
long as they are employed by or under them, all
fuch perfons fhall be admitted members of this
Society without any exception, provided fuch
perfons as are now ferving as aforefaid, and above
that age, be entered in the Society within three
calendar months after the firft monthly meeting;
and that all other perfons under forty-five years
of age, that may hereafter be bound apprentices,
or hired in fuch manner as to gain fettlements in
the parifh of C. E. be entered into this Society
within three months after fuch binding, hiring,
or attaining the age of ten years.

Women may
be admitted,
and become
entitled to
annuities.

34. That any woman under the age of forty-
five years may be admitted into this Society, fo
as to be entitled to annuities in the claffes and
manner herein before fpecified; but fuch women
fhall not in any cafe be entitled to receive any
weekly allowances for ficknefs or infirmity; nor
fhall they be liable to ferve any office, or be fined
for non-attendance at the yearly meetings.

Benefits for
children.

35. That any member of this Society wifhing
to make a provifion for his children under twelve
years of age, may be allowed to enter fuch of
them as he may think proper on the following
terms:

If under four years of age when admitted, to
pay four-pence monthly for each child, till it
attain twelve years of age, if the member fo long
live;

If four years and under feven years of age when
admitted, to pay three-pence monthly for each
child;

If feven years and under ten years of age
when

when admitted, to pay two-pence monthly for each child.

If any fuch member, fo contributing for his children, fhall die, and leave any child or children under twelve years of age, one fhilling a week fhall be applied out of the funds of this Society, towards the maintenance of each child fo contributed for, till it attain the age of twelve years; but no child fhall be entitled to any benefit unlefs entered and paid for twelve calendar months before fuch member's death; and any member choofing to contribute double the above-mentioned fums fhall be allowed fo to do, and in that cafe the children fhall be entitled to double allowances in cafe of the father's death as afore-faid *.

36. That

---

* The contributions for children may be thought rather low in proportion to the fum to be paid; but the chance of the child's dying in its father's life-time, or afterwards under twelve years of age, and alfo the greater probability of the father's living, is to be calculated. But fuppofing the contributions to be too low, it is a very ufeful application of a part of the fund. Not many of the members of this Society have availed themfelves of the opportunity of entering their children, but the recent death of one of its members (fee p. 60) leaving two children entitled to relief will, it is expected, induce many others to fecure for their infant children a comfortable fupport, in cafe of the member's death. The form of entry of children is bound in a book, and is as follows: " I, D. E. of   in
" the parifh of   and county of   and a
" member of the Caftle Eden Friendly Society, do requeft that
" my (fon or daughter) A. E. may be entered into that Society ;
" for whom I intend to pay to the treafurer of the faid So-
" ciety for the time being   pence on every fourth Saturday
" from the day of h   entrance, until he (or fhe) attain the age
" of twelve years; which will be on the   day of
" in the year of our Lord   if I and   he fo long do live.
                                                        " Witnefs

Power to ap-
point a fur-
geon.

36. That the fteward, directors, and committee, fhall, if they think proper, agree with
fome apothecary or furgeon, to attend all the
members of this Society within the faid parifhes,
or fuch of them as they may think neceffary;
which apothecary or furgeon fhall report to the
fteward for the time being, his opinion on each
fuch member's cafe; and the fteward, directors,
and committee, fhall order fuch fum or fums to
be paid for fuch attendance as they may think
proper, not exceeding one penny per week for
each member *

To provide
books,

37. That the fteward, directors, and committee,
fhall, from time to time, provide all fuch books,
chefts, and other things as they may think neceffary for this Society, and order the treafurer to

and pay fa-
laries, &c.

pay for the fame out of the fund; and fhall alfo
order fuch falary or falaries and allowances to be
paid to the clerks and treafurer, as they may from
time to time think right and neceffary, which
falaries and allowances fhall not in any cafe ex-

" Witnefs my hand, this   day of   in the year
" of our Lord   " D. E."
    " Be it remembered, that the above-named A. E. was this
"   day of   in the year of our Lord
" duly entered into the Caftle Eden Friendly Society, and if h
" father continue to make the faid monthly payments during
" his life, he will be entitled to   fhillings a week out
" of the fund of this Society, from the death of h   faid
" father until the faid   day of   thoufand
"   hundred   if he fo long live.
                        " M. S. Steward.
                        " W. M. Clerk."

* A furgeon was appointed *(fee Proceedings,* p. 53), with
a falary of ten pounds *per annum,* in addition to which many
of the members agreed to contribute after the rate of a halfpenny *per* week to procure medicines and fave the fund.

ceed

ceed five *per cent.* on the contributions received * ;
but no allowance fhall be made to the fteward, directors, or committee, for their trouble.

38. That every member of this Society fhall Yearly
meeting.
meet on the firft day of January yearly, unlefs it
fhould fall on a Sunday, and in that cafe on the
day before, at fuch houfe within the parifh of C. E.
as the fteward, directors, and committee, fhall
appoint, at the hour of ten in the forenoon, and
anfwer to his name when called, and then pay to
the treafurer one fhilling for dinner and liquor:
at which meeting the members fhall nominate and Appoint-
elect by ballot a committee of twelve difcreet and ment of com-
mittee,
honeft members, refiding and inhabiting within the
faid parifhes, who underftand accounts and are
able to write, and who fhall be above the age of
twenty-one years; which committee fhall continue in office until the next yearly meeting †, unlefs they or any of them fhall die,
or refufe to act, or remove out of the faid parifhes, or be excluded this Society. At the annual and vifitors.
meeting alfo fhall be elected fix vifitors for the
year enfuing.

39. That at all elections for ftewards, directors, Abfent
or committees, the members of this Society may members
may vote by
(when they are fick, abfent, or cannot conveniently proxy.
attend any general or yearly meeting) depute and
appoint a proxy or deputy, being a member of
this Society, to vote for them refpectively, provided fuch appointment be in writing, and figned
by the member or members fo appointing, and be
produced to, and left with the clerks of the Society at the time of voting; but no one member

---

* The falaries, allowances, &c. to clerks, treafurers, &c.
have not amounted to $1\frac{1}{2}$ *per cent.* on the contributions received
fince the eftablifhment of the Society.

† Altered. *(See* p. 47.)

fhall

F

fhall be proxy, or vote for more than fix abfent members *.

Power to make new rules. 40. That at each yearly meeting the fteward, directors, and committee, fhall acquaint the members with their proceedings during the laft year, and explain the ftate of the funds; and the accounts fhall undergo fuch infpection as this Society, at fuch yearly meeting, fhall direct †: and it being almoft impoffible, in the infancy of fuch an eftablifhment, to form rules which will apply to every cafe that may arife relative to the regulation of the Society, and the management of its funds, it fhall be lawful at each yearly meeting, with the concurrence and approbation of three-fourths of the members of this Society then prefent, to frame new rules, orders, and regulations, provided a requifition for that purpofe, figned by three or more of the members, fhall have been read publicly at two monthly meetings, held next before fuch yearly meeting: but no new rule, order, or regulation, fhall be binding, until the fame fhall have been agreed to and confirmed by feven directors at the leaft, and the fteward of this Society for the time being, and alfo confirmed by the juftices of the peace in manner directed by the faid act of par-

Duration. liament. Nor fhall it be lawful to diffolve this Society, or to make any divifion or diftribution of the ftock or fund, or of any part thereof, contrary to the true intent and meaning of thefe

* To prevent too much influence being given to any one member.

† By a refolution of a yearly meeting *(fee* p. 56), two honorary members, and the fteward for the time being, are appointed auditors, to examine the accounts between the laft monthly meeting and the yearly meeting.

Refolu-

Refolutions, Rules, Orders, and Regulations, with
out the confent and approbation of five-fixths of
the then exifting members, and alfo of all perfons
then receiving, or entitled to receive relief from
this Society, either on account of ficknefs, age, or
infirmity, fuch confent and approbation to be
teftified under their hands individually; nor
without the approbation of feven directors at the
leaft, and the fteward of this Society for the
time being, and alfo of the juftices of the peace
in manner directed by the faid act of parliament.

41. That all the rules, orders, and regulations, Rules to be
made from time to time by this Society in manner entered in a
herein before directed, fhall be forthwith entered pened for
in a book or books to be kept for that purpofe by infpection.
the fteward for the time being, and be figned by
the members, directors, and fteward, or fo many
of them as herein before provided, and fhall at all
feafonable times be open for the infpection of any
member of this Society; and fuch rules, orders,
and regulations, fo entered and figned, fhall be
deemed original orders, and be received as fuch
in all difputes which relate to this Society.

42. That each member of this Society fhall Members
be entitled to a certificate under the hands of the entitled to a
fteward and treafurer for the time being, for the
purpofes mentioned in the faid act, on demand,
and on paying fixpence to the clerk *.

43. That

---

* The Society's certificates are in many cafes very ufeful, and prevent the members being removed until actually
chargeable. In the inftance of unmarried women having children in a parifh to which they do not belong, the Society's certificate will be a better fecurity than many bonds of indemnity:
queftions alfo of fettlement may be decided without the removal
of the certificated perfon under the faid act, 33 Geo. III. c. 54.
§ 21, 22. It is to be obferved, that the act of parliament re-

quires

What orders are valid. 43. That no order, act, or deed of the steward, directors, and committee, shall be deemed sufficient or valid, unless the steward (or any three of the trustees for the time being), three of the

---

quires " such certificate to be under the hands of the stewards, " presidents, wardens, or treasurers of such Societies, or any " two of them for the time being, to be attested by one or " more credible witness or witnesses ;" therefore certificates under the hands of the steward and clerk will not be sufficient. The following is a copy of the form used by this Society :

" To all whom it may concern.

" Castle Eden Friendly Society. We, " of Castle Eden, in the county of Durham, steward of the " said Society, and   of Castle Eden aforesaid, " treasurer of the said Society, in pursuance of authority given " unto us by an act of parliament made and passed in the thirty- " third year of the reign of his Majesty King George the Third, " intituled, ' An Act for the encouragement and relief of " ' Friendly Societies,' do hereby certify, own, and acknowledge, " that   of   in the parish of " " in the county of " is a member of the said Society.

" In witness whereof we have hereunto set our hands, this " day of   in the year of our Lord one " thousand   hundred

Steward.

" Attested by   Treasurer."

" I,   one of his Majesty's " justices of the peace in and for the county of Durham, do " hereby certify, that   one of the wit- " nesses who attested the above certificate, hath this day made " oath before me, that he the said   did see the said " " and   the steward and treasurer " of the said Society, whose names are subscribed above, seve- " rally sign the same ; and that the names of the said " " and   who are " the witnesses attesting the said certificate, are respectively of " their own proper hand-writing.

" Given under my hand, this   day of " in the year of our Lord one thousand   hundred

directors,

directors, and feven of the committee, at the leaft, confent to and fign the fame; but that all fuch orders, acts, and deeds of fuch fteward (or any three of the truftees for the time being), directors, and committee, fhall be deemed the orders, acts, and deeds of the Society at large, and fhall have the fame effect as if agreed to and figned by the whole. And that in all cafes where the confent or fignature of the fteward is required, the confent and fignature of any three of the truftees for the time being fhall be equivalent to the confent of the fteward.

44. That every benevolent perfon who fhall contribute five pounds or upwards, in one pay-ment, as an encouragement to this Society, fhall be entitled to act as a director during his life; or any perfon that fhall fubfcribe five fhil-lings a quarter, fhall be entitled (fo long as he fhall continue to pay fuch fubfcription) to act as a director,—no regard being had to refidence; and all fuch contributors and fubfcribers, in con-fequence of their not receiving any benefit from the Society, fhall be denominated honorary mem-bers: and all fuch fums fhall be applied to the general purpofes of this Society, in like manner as the contributions of the feveral members. *Honorary members.*

And laftly, Refolved unanimoufly,

That thefe Refolutions, Rules, Orders, and Re-gulations, be figned for and in behalf of this meeting by the chairman, and counterfigned by the clerks, and twenty others, who are to be ad-mitted members.

(Signed)   M. S. Chairman.
(Counterfigned)   T. P.
                        W. M. } Clerks.
                        G. O. J. G.
                        &c. &c.

D. *(to wit.) At the general quarter seffions of the peace, holden at the city of Durham, in and for the faid county, &c. &c.*

The Refolutions, Rules, Orders, and Regulations, contained in this and the preceding pages, and alfo a duplicate thereof on parchment, were exhibited to the juftices of the peace, affembled at this adjourned feffion, and, after due examination thereof, allowed and confirmed.

(Signed)   R. O. ⎫
                R. R. ⎬ Juftices of the peace.
                R. B. ⎭

                G. P. Clerk of the peace.

Specimen of the Mode of refcinding and altering Rules, &c.

C. E. County of D.   179

At the yearly meeting of the members of the C. E. Friendly Society, held here this day in purfuance of the 38th article of the Rules, Orders, and Regulations for the government and guidance of that Society, which were allowed and confirmed by his Majefty's juftices of the peace for the faid county, at the general quarter feffions of the peace, holden at the city of D. the day of under the authority of an Act of Parliament paffed on the twenty-firft day of June 1793, intituled, " An Act for the " encouragement and relief of Friendly So- " cieties;"

Refolved unanimoufly, That the following alterations in the faid Refolutions, Rules, Orders, and Regulations fhall be made, and that the fame
fh al

ſhall take effect and be binding on all the members of this Society, in the ſame manner as if the original Rules, Orders, and Regulations had been ſo made, from the time the ſame ſhall have been agreed to and confirmed by the directors, ſteward, and juſtices of the peace in manner directed by the 3d ſection of the ſaid Act of Parliament, and the 40th article of the ſaid Rules, Orders, and Regulations (a proper requiſition for theſe alterations having been publicly read at the two laſt monthly meetings of the ſaid Society) ; that is to ſay :

1ſt. That a part of the 25th article, which di-" rects the ſaid annuities to be paid by monthly " payments at each monthly meeting," ſhall be reſcinded ; and inſtead of it the following ſhall be ſubſtituted :

The ſaid annual annuities to be paid by quarterly payments on the laſt monthly meeting in March, June, September, and December.

2d. That part of the 28th article, which declares that " no member ſhall be obliged to ſerve " in ſuch committee two years together," ſhall be reſcinded, and inſtead thereof the following ſhall be ſubſtituted :

That no member ſhall be obliged to ſerve in ſuch committee three years together.

In confirmation of the Reſolutions, Rules, Orders, and Regulations immediately preceding, and in teſtimony of their being duly made and agreed to at this yearly or general meeting, held the   day of   we have hereunto ſubſcribed our names (and alſo to a duplicate of the ſame on parchment), being above three-fourths of the members preſent at the ſaid meeting.

(Signatures.)

We whoſe names are hereunto ſubſcribed, being the

the fteward and directors of the C. E. Friendly
Society, having duly examined the Refolutions,
Rules, Orders, and Regulations preceding, do
hereby agree to and confirm the fame, this
day of
Signed by the fteward and directors.

Durham (to wit). *At the general quarter feffions
of the peace, holden at the city of Durham, in
and for the faid county, on Wednefday the
day of in the year of our Lord
before*

The Refolutions, Rules, Orders, and Regulations made and agreed to at the yearly meeting
aforefaid, and alfo a duplicate thereof on parchment, were exhibited to the juftices of the peace
affembled at this general feffion, and after due
examination thereof allowed and confirmed.

J. E. ⎫
R. O. ⎬ Juftices of the peace.
R. B. ⎭

G. P. Clerk of the peace *.

---

* Sir F. Eden obferves, in his State of the Poor, vol. ii.
p. 226, that the expenfe attending an application to the
juftices is the common reafon given why four of the Friendly Societies in Portfea, Hampfhire, have not had their Rules confirmed ; and in p. 655 he obferves, that fome of the Friendly Societies in Wolverhampton thought that the application to the
quarter feffions would be expenfive. This appears extraordinary,
it being enacted in the 2d fect. of 33 Geo. III. ch. 54. that all
" fuch Rules, Orders, and Regulations, fo confirmed, fhall be
" figned by the clerk of the peace at fuch feffions, and a dupli-
" cate thereof, being firft fairly written on parchment, fhall be
" depofited with the clerk of the peace at fuch feffions, to be by
" him filed with the rolls of the feffion there *without any fee* to
" be paid for any matter or thing relating to the fame."

CONTENTS

CONTENTS of PROCEEDINGS.

G

1796, *Dec.* 31. *Refolution that no perfon ferve longer than two years together in committee.*
New committee-men and vifitors to be propofed by their predeceffors.
Refolution of thanks.
Do. for printing a ftatement of accounts, &c.
Order for holding next monthly meeting.

1797, *Jan.* 21. *Information of alterations in Rules having been confirmed.*

Oct. 28. *Information of the death of J. D. a member.*
Order for payment of money to his widow and children.
Refolution of thanks to the members who attended his funeral.
Regulations concerning funerals.

Nov. 25. *Propofition for making fome allowance on the death of a member's wife.*

Dec. 23. *Propofing of committee and vifitors.*
Order for treafurer and clerk's allowance.

1798, *Jan.* 1. *Yearly meeting.*
Information of laft year's proceedings.
Election of committee-men and vifitors.
Refolution of thanks, &c.

Extracts from the Proceedings, as Specimens.

AT the houfe of G. T. innkeeper in C. E. in the county of D. on   the   day of
in the   year of the reign of   and in the year of our Lord   being the fourth Saturday after the Refolutions, Rules, Orders, and Regulations, for the government of the C. E. Friendly Society, had been allowed and confirmed by the juftices of the peace for the faid county, at their quarter feffions, as directed by an act of parliament made and paffed in the year 1793, entitled, " An Act, &c." the fteward, directors, and committee, after qualifying *, proceeded to carry the faid Refolutions, Rules, Orders, and Regulations, into execution.

Ordered—That the treafurer, Mr. G. T. fhall, agreeably to the 11th article, deliver to the Society a bond, from himfelf and two other fureties (to be deemed fufficient), in the penal fum of two hundred pounds.

The faid G. T. agreeably to the above order, delivered to this Society a bond †, from himfelf, T. T. and W. L. in the penal fum of two hundred pounds, payable to the clerk of the peace for the faid county, for the faithful execution of his office; which bond is hereby accepted as fufficient, and the fteward is defired to keep the fame in truft for the Society until further orders.

The members of the firft and fecond claffes of the old C. E. Friendly Society, having refolved to incorporate themfelves with this Society, and

---

* *See Form of Declaration,* p. 17.
† *See Form of Bond,* p. 13.

having

having transferred all their ftock and funds into the ftock and funds of this Society, they, amongft the following perfons, were duly admitted members hereof. See their refpective declarations *.

No. 1. M. S. of C. E. One fhare.
  2. G. O. of C. E. blackfmith, One fhare.
  3. J. G. of C. E. Half a fhare.

Ordered by the directors prefent, that G. O. one of the committee, do keep one of the keys.

  Signed by the fteward, three directors, and twelve committee-men.

At a monthly Meeting held at   *5th Oct.* 1793.

The following perfons were propofed to become members at the next monthly meeting, and a depofit of two fhillings and fixpence for each was paid to the treafurer accordingly:

  W. C. of B. cordwainer, by L. D.
  W. B. of S. joiner, by M. W.
  J. S. of C. E. labourer, by do.

At this meeting alfo, J. D. one of the members, entered two of his children †, viz.

  M. D. aged two years on 10th Feb. laft.
  B. D. born 27th March laft.

  Signed by the fteward, four directors, and nine committee-men.

At a monthly Meeting held at   *2d Nov.* 1793.

The perfons propofed at the laft monthly meeting were duly admitted members, viz.

No. 91, W. C No. 92, W. B. No. 93, J. S.

  Signed by the fteward, three directors, and nine committee-men.

---

* *See Form of Declaration,* p. 17.
† *See Form of Entry,* p. 39.

At a monthly Meeting held at 25th *Jan.* 1794.

Refolved—That Mr. M. R. of S. fhall be, and he is hereby appointed furgeon and apothecary to this Society, to attend the members when fick, and report their cafes to the fteward, with a falary of ten pounds *per annum* *.

Ordered—That the treafurer pay unto A. B. of D. Efq. twenty pounds, part of the money belonging to this Society, for which he is to receive a promiffory note payable on demand to R. B. Efq. the Rev. H. M. and the Rev. D. H. three of the truftees for this Society, bearing intereft after the rate of four pounds ten fhillings *per cent. per ann.*

That the treafurer for the time being fhall receive the interefts to become due on this, and all other fecurities belonging to the Society, until further orders, and that the truftees do give orders accordingly.

That Mr. J. W. of C. E. be, and he is hereby appointed treafurer of this Society, agreeable to the 36th article, in the room of Mr. G. T.; and that he do, agreeable the 11th article, deliver to the fteward a bond, from himfelf, and two fufficient fureties, in the penal fum of two hundred pounds, before the next monthly meeting.

Signed by the fteward, three directors, and eight committee-men.

At a monthly Meeting held at G. T.'s, 22d *Feb.* 1794.

Mr. J. W. the new treafurer, delivered to the fteward a bond, agreeable to the order of laft meeting, executed by himfelf, R. W. and G. O.; which this meeting accepts as fufficient.

---

* *See* p. 40.

Ordered,

Ordered, That G. T. the old treasurer, do deliver to J. W. the new treasurer, the chests, money, securities, and every other thing in his possession belonging to the Society.

Resolved, That this meeting do now adjourn to the house of J. W. and that the meetings of the Society be there held until ordered to the contrary.

Signed by the steward, three directors, and seven committee-men.

At a monthly Meeting held at   21*st Feb.* 1795.

Proof having been made to this meeting that R. W. a member of this Society, having three shares (No. 25, 81, 82), died at Fort Royal in the West Indies on the 8th day of June last, without leaving widow, child, or children, and without making any appointment in writing;

Ordered, That the treasurer do pay unto the legal representatives of the said R. W. five pounds, due to them by the 24th article, for the share No. 25, and eleven shillings, due to them by the 18th article, for the same share, being the proportionable part of the payments in advance for that share, since the said 8th June; and also that he do pay unto the said representatives two pounds ten shillings, due to them by the 26th article, being the full amount of what has been paid into the funds of this Society for the said shares, Nos. 81 and 82.

Ordered, That the members do pay at the next monthly meeting six-pence for each share, and three-pence for each half share, agreeable to the 17th article, towards reimbursing the said five pounds.

Signed by the steward, five directors, and ten committee-men.

At

At a monthly Meeting, held the 18th April 1795.

Ordered, That the treasurer do pay G. R. twelve shillings for two weeks sickness *

Ordered, That a general meeting of this Society be holden at the next monthly meeting, at six o'clock in the evening, for the purpose of electing a proper person as one of the committee (agreeable to the 14th article), in the room of W. L. who has left the three parishes.

Signed by the steward, three directors, and ten committee-men.

––––––––––

At a general Meeting, held the 16th of May 1795, in pursuance of an Order made at the last monthly Meeting, and of the 14th Article, for the Purpose of electing a proper Person as one of the Committee in the Room of W. L.

T. H. and T. N. both of C. E. were proposed. On the close of the ballot T. H. had a majority of seventeen, and, being declared duly elected, he made the declaration required by the thirteenth article.

Signed by the steward.

––––––––––

At a yearly Meeting, held at the C. E. Inn, the 1st Jan. 1796.

The steward informed the Society of the proceedings of the committee, &c. during the last year, agreeably to the direction of the fortieth article, and that the money out at interest and in the

––––––––––––––––––––

* By the 21st article, the steward is empowered to order payment for the weekly allowances in sickness; but it is usual in this Society to make the orders at monthly meetings, so that the members may be better informed of the disbursements of the Society.

chest

cheſt amounted to 316*l*. 8*s*. 5½*d*. and the net ſavings of the laſt year to 111*l*. 5*s*. 11*d*.

Reſolved unanimouſly, That the honorary members, or any two of them, and the ſteward for the time being, ſhall be, and they are hereby appointed ſtanding auditors of the Society's accounts, agreeably to the fortieth article, and the allowance of the accounts under their hands ſhall be deemed ſufficient; and they ſhall be annually requeſted, immediately after the laſt monthly meeting in December, to audit the accounts, and report the ſtate thereof at the then next yearly meeting.

That the ſteward, directors, and committee, for the time being, be requeſted to lend out of the fund of this Society to any of the members of this Society reſident within the pariſhes of C. E. E. and M. H. a ſum of money not exceeding ten pounds, nor leſs than five pounds, to be laid out in the purchaſing of a cow, to be kept within one of the aforeſaid three pariſhes, for the uſe of ſuch member's family, on his giving to the Society a ſufficient promiſſory note ſigned by himſelf, and other two houſeholders within the ſaid pariſhes, for the repayment of ſuch ſum of money, with legal intereſt *.

Signed by the ſteward.

At

* The lending of money for the purpoſe of purchaſing cows has been found beneficial in the pariſh of Caſtle Eden; for within two years eight cows have been purchaſed; the members have in general paid their inſtalments regularly, and ſome the whole of the money lent. It was thought better to have a diſcretionary power in the ſteward, directors, and committee, for lending ſuch ſums, than to make it a matter of right. If the Legiſlature ſhould exempt members of Friendly Societies, formed upon certain approved plans, from the payment of poor rates for their houſes, gardens, and ground for cow-keeping, under

At a monthly Meeting held at 19*th March* 1796.

Ordered, That the fum of ten pounds be lent to T. N. for the purpofe of purchafing a cow, and that the treafurer do advance the fame, on his receiving a promiffory note figned by the faid T. N. and J. A. and J. B. bearing intereft after the rate of five *per cent. per ann.*

Refolved, That the faid T. N. fhall be at liberty to repay the faid ten pounds and intereft by inftalments of ten fhillings at each monthly meeting.

W. G. was excluded the benefit of this Society for non-payment of his contribution at this and the two preceding meetings.

G. T. a member, for one fhare, No. 14, was admitted to a fecond fhare (No. 121), agreeable to the thirty fecond article.

Only fix of the committee having voted in favour of W. J. who was propofed at the laft monthly meeting to become a member; Ordered, That the two fhillings and fixpence paid for his depofit be returned.

Signed by the fteward, three directors, and ten committee-men.

At a monthly Meeting held the 6*th Nov.* 1796.

The members prefent at this meeting having taken into confideration the Refolutions, Rules, Orders, and Regulations, for the government and guidance of this Society, It was refolved, That a requifition be made to the next yearly meeting for making the following alterations, viz.

---

under fpecific rents and regulations, it would tend much to encourage thefe eftablifhments, and to increafe the comforts of the labouring part of the community.

1ft. That a part of the 25th article, which directs " the faid annuities to be paid by monthly " payments at each monthly meeting" fhall be refcinded; and inftead of which the following fhall be fubftituted:

The faid annuities to be paid by quarterly payments on the laft monthly meeting in March, June, September, and December.

2d. That a part of the 28th article, which declares, that " no member fhall be obliged to ferve " in fuch committee two years together," fhall be refcinded; and inftead thereof the following fhall be fubftituted:

That no member fhall be obliged to ferve in fuch committee three years together.

Thefe refolutions were publicly read, and notice given, as required by the 3d fection of the act of parliament for the Encouragement and Relief of Friendly Societies, and of the 40th article or rule of this Society, and fubfcribed by the eleven following members.

Signed by eleven members.

At a monthly Meeting held at   the 24th Dec. 1796.

The refolutions and notices of the laft monthly meeting were read and approved by the members prefent.

Ordered, That the treafurer pay unto Mr. M. R. five pounds, for half year's attendance as furgeon and apothecary.

Signed by the fteward, three directors,
and nine of the committee.

At a yearly Meeting, held at the Houfe of G. T. *the* 31ft *Dec.* 1796.

A ftatement of the accounts, figned by the auditors (as appointed at the laft yearly meeting),
was

was read, by which the Society was informed, that the money at intereſt and in the cheſt amounted to 462*l.* 16*s.* 0½*d.*, and the net ſavings of the year to 146*l.* 7*s.* 7*d.*

The proceedings of the two laſt monthly meetings were read, and a requiſition made that the alterations of the Rules, Orders, and Regulations of the Society, propoſed at the monthly meeting held on the 26th Nov. laſt, ſhould be agreed to and confirmed. After duly conſidering the ſame, It was unanimouſly reſolved, That the ſame alterations ſhall be made, and the reſolutions copied in the bye law, and the duplicate on parchment ſhall be now ſigned and confirmed by the members *.

That the directors and ſteward, and the juſtices of the peace for this county, be requeſted to agree to and confirm the ſame.

At this meeting J. G., J. U., P. K., J. A., J. U., and J. N., were re-elected to ſerve in the committee for the year eufuing; and M. O., G. O., J. M., J. M., J. B, M. D. and T L. were elected by ballot to ſerve in the committee for two years enſuing.

That each of the ſix old committee-men who ſhall go out of office, and each of the ſix viſitors, ſhall annually at the laſt monthly meeting in December recommend two proper perſons, one of which the yearly meeting may elect as his ſucceſſor.

That theſe reſolutions, with a ſtatement of the accounts, from the commencement of the Society (Auguſt 10th, 1793) to this time, and a ſhort abſtract of the members' contributions and benefits, be

---

* *See* pp. 46, 47, 48.

H 2   printed;

printed; and that copies be fent by the fteward to the Rev. Mr. H. the honorary members, the principal proprietors of lands, and other ladies and gentlemen interefted, in the parifhes of C. E. E. and M. H.

Ordered by the fteward, directors, and committee, That the next monthly meeting fhall be holden at the houfe of

Signed by the fteward, feven directors, and nine of the committee.

At a monthly Meeting held at 21ſt *Jan.* 1797.

This meeting was informed that the alterations in the Rules, Orders, and Regulations agreed to at the laft yearly meeting had been duly confirmed by the directors and fteward, and alfo by the juftices of the peace at the quarter feffions held in Durham on the 11th inftant.

The directors appointed M. O. (one of the committee), agreeable to the 19th article, to keep one of the keys, in lieu of T. H.

Signed by the fteward, three directors, and twelve of the committee.

At a monthly Meeting held the 28*th* Oct. 1797.

This meeting was informed that J. D. a member of this Society, for one fhare (No. 7), died on Saturday the 21ft of this month, and was buried at E. the Monday following.

Ordered, That the treafurer do pay unto his widow, J. D. five pounds, as directed by the 24th article, and eighteen fhillings for three weeks ficknefs, due on the day of his death; alfo two fhillings for one week's allowance for her fon B. D. and daughter M. D. to be applied towards their maintenance, agreeable to the 35th article;
and

and that the treafurer for the time being do pay
monthly after the rate of one fhilling for each
child, until they refpectively attain twelve years
of age; that is to fay, for M. D. until the 10th
February 1803, and for B. D. until the 27th
March 1805, if they fo long live *.

That all the members of this Society be _re-
quefted_ † to attend the funerals of fuch members as may die and be buried in their refpective parifhes; and that when any member fhall
die within the parifhes of C. E. E. or M. H. the vifitors fhall give notice to the members refident
within fuch parifh of the time of the funeral; and
in order to prevent confufion, that the following
regulations be adopted, unlefs the friends of the
deceafed do fignify their requeft to the contrary,
viz. eight of the prefent or paft committee fhall

---

* The Society will have to pay for thofe children thirty-four
pounds nine fhillings, for which the father contributed only one
pound fourteen fhillings and eight-pence.

† It is thought beft only to recommend the attending of
funerals, as fubjecting the members to fines for non-attendance in many cafes prevents young men from becoming members, their bufinefs rendering fuch attendance inconvenient.

The benefits paid to a member on the lofs of his wife in moft
Societies, appear to be on an unequal principle with refpect to
unmarried members, and in many cafes prevent the moft eligible
perfons from becoming members. When the funds of Friendly
Societies continue increafing, many of the members fuppofe they
are contributing after too high a rate, and confequently propofe
either to diminifh the contributions, or to charge the Society
with additional payments; not, however, calculating the demands
which will be made when the members grow old. To fhow the
members of this Society the neceffity of adhering to the Rules, a
Table has been publifhed _(fee_ p. 29). The contributions of
few Societies will bear to be lowered, but it is to be feared, that
many will find the neceffity of increafing them, or, what will be
worfe, of diminifhing their propofed benefits.

act

act as pall-bearers; and for want of that number, the oldeft members prefent fhall fupply their places, and four or fix of the youngeft members prefent (if others be not provided) be under-bearers. The vifitors to follow the coffin as mourners, and the reft of the members prefent to walk two and two before the coffin; junior members firft. The treafurer to fee the expenfe of the coffin, burial fees, &c. paid out of the allowance from the Society.

Signed by the fteward, five directors, and eleven of the committee.

At a monthly Meeting held the 25th Nov. 1797.

It was propofed that a requifition fhould be made to the next yearly meeting for an alteration in the Rules, fo that an allowance might be made out of the funds of this Society, at the death of each member's wife, to be applied towards her funeral; but the meeting confidering it to be improper to charge the fund with a payment for which no provifion had been made by the original articles, and that members have, under the prefent Rules, an opportunity of contributing for their wives, and by that means of fecuring an allowance at their death, the propofition was withdrawn.

At a monthly Meeting held the 23d Dec. 1797.

The following perfons were propofed, in purfuance of a refolution of the laft yearly meeting, by the fix old committee-men, as proper perfons for their fucceffors, for two years enfuing, viz.

W. C. and E. D. by J. G.

R. J and M. B. by J. B.

T. B.

T. B. and J. O. by J. W.
G. T. and W. K. by J. W.
J. B. and W. J. by J. A.
G. A. and S. W. by J. N.

And the following were propofed by the vifitors as proper perfons for their fucceffors for the year enfuing, viz.

W. T. and J. L. by R. C.
J. R. and J. A. by J. R.
T. G. and J. U. by P. S.
T. R. and W. E. by J. T.
J. B. and W. T. by T. T.
R. H. and S. B. by J. L.

Ordered, That G. T. be paid two pounds five fhillings for ale, at nine monthly meetings; and that he be paid one pound one fhilling as a compenfation for the ufe of the room, fire, candles, &c. and that the clerks be paid two guineas for one year's falary *

Signed by the fteward, four directors, and ten of the committee.

At a yearly Meeting held at the C. E. Inn the 1ft of Jan. 1798.

Prefent, four truftees, eleven directors, and one hundred and twenty-five members.

The fteward informed this meeting of the proceedings of the committee during the laft year, and the auditor's report was read, by which it appeared that the money out at intereft and in the cheft amounted to five hundred and fixty-feven pounds nineteen fhillings, and the net favings of laft year to one hundred and five pounds two fhillings and eleven-pence halfpenny.

In addition to M. O., G. O., J. M., J. B., M. D., and T. S., the fix old committee-men, the

---

* *See Note,* p. 16.

following were elected by ballot as new committee-men for two years enfuing, viz.

E. D., G. T., M. B., J. B., T. B., and S. W

And the following were appointed vifitors for
the year enfuing, viz.

W. T. and W. E. for the parifh of C. E.

J. U. and R. H. for the parifh of E.

J. R. and J. B. for the parifh of M. H.

Refolved unanimoufly, That the thanks of the
Society be given to the Rev. J— B—, M. A. for his
fermon ; to the honorary members for their
fubfcriptions ; and to the fteward, directors, and
other officers for their trouble.

That a table of the fums payable to annuitants
be printed, fhowing the amount which may be
received for one fhare from fifty to ninety-five
years of age ; as it is prefumed that the benefits to
arife from the annuities, if better underftood,
would induce men to fubfcribe for their wives, and
thereby fecure to them a comfortable fupport in
old age *.

That thefe refolutions, with abftracts of the
accounts, and the auditors' report, be printed, and
fent to the honorary members ; and that copies
thereof, with the laft year's ftatement of contributions and benefits, be alfo fent, by the fteward, to
fuch ladies and gentlemen interefted in the parifhes
of C. E. E. and M. H. and the neighbouring town-
fhips, as have not already favoured the Society with
their fubfcriptions ; the members hoping that its
principles and objects are fuch, as, when known,
will not fail to fecure the honour of their pa-
tronage.

That the fteward do fign thefe refolutions in the
name of the meeting.

M. S. Steward.

* *See* p. 28.

Schedule

Schedule of Books kept by the Society.

I. Bye-law Book, kept by the ſteward, in purſuance of the 41ſt Art. in which are the original and ſubſequent Rules allowed by the magiſtrates, bound up with the Act of Parliament for encouraging Friendly Societies.

II. Order Book, into which are copied all the Rules and the Proceedings of the Society, from which the Extracts, p. 51 to 64, are taken.

III. Officers' Declarations. See p. 17.

IV. Members' Declarations. See p. 25.

V. Entrances of Members' Children. See p. 38, 39.

VI. Monthly Contributions.

VII. Diſburſements for Sickneſs, Annuities, Children, &c.

VIII. Members' Ledger.

IX. General Ledger, in which are contained,

The Treaſurer's Account of all Money received and paid.

Separate Accounts of each Perſon to whom Money is lent.

Donations and Subſcriptions.

Dividends and Intereſts.

Entrances, Fines, Salaries, &c. (which ſerves as a profit and loſs account.)

Annual Balances of Members' Accounts.

General Balance, which is taken annually, and examined and ſigned by the auditors.

F I N I S.

RULES AND REGULATIONS

TO BE OBSERVED

BY THE

SOCIETY AT ANNAN,

CALLED

The Trades Society,

AS APPROVED OF, AND CONFIRMED BY,

THE QUARTER SESSIONS

HELD AT ANNAN

ON THE SECOND OF JUNE,

One Thousand Eight Hundred and One.

DUMFRIES,

Printed at the

St. Michael Press,

BY

C. M'LACHLAN,
1801,

LAWS AND REGULATIONS

OF THE

TRADES SOCIETY

AT

A N N A N.

Reasons for forming the Society.

FROM a confideration of the utility of *Societies* in general—the uncertainty of worldly profperity—the calamities—misfortunes—and troubles HUMAN LIFE is liable to, WE have refolved to form ourfelves into a Friendly Society, called the *ANNAN TRADES SOCIETY*, for the purpofe of employing a fmall portion of our own means and incomes towards raifing a Fund for our mutual relief, agreeable to the following ARTICLES.

ARTICLE I.

Qualifications of perfons applying for admission—Mode of application for admission.

THAT every perfon who fhall be admitted a Member of this Society be of good repute, and of a fober life, and known to be fo by at leaft one of the prefent Members: None fhall be admitted, if objected to by a majority; nor any who fhall be deemed in a declining ftate of health, or upwards of thirty-fix years of age. And any perfon who wifhes to become a Member of this Society muft be recom-

mended a quarter before his being admitted. And every
person who shall be admitted a Member, shall subscribe the
minute of his admission thereby becoming bound to observe
all the Articles of the Society.

II.
Crimes for which Members are liable to be excluded.

THAT if any Member shall be found to allow himself in a
wicked course of life, or conversation unsuitable to his pro-
fession, or shall be guilty of any enormous crime—such as
murder, theft, robbery, or the like, or crimes of any kind
punishable by the law of this country, he shall, upon this
being proved to the satisfaction of the Society, be forthwith
excluded.

III.
Day and hour of meeting—Office-bearers elected.

THAT the Society shall hold a General Meeting on the
twenty-fifth day of June annually or Thursay thereafter;—
the hour of meeting to be precisely at eleven o'clock in the
forenoon, when the Society are to have a Procession or Sermon; and four o'clock in the afternoon when there is no
Procession or Sermon: At which meeting the Society shall
elect a Preses, two Box-masters, a Clerk, Officer, and Stand-
ard-bearer, for the ensuing year, by a majority of votes;
and any person refusing to serve in said offices, shall be fined
in the sum of *two shillings* and *sixpence,* to be paid the
next meeting, on pain of *exclusion.*

IV.
Election of the Committee, and their allowance—Attendance of Members within ten miles—Qurterly meeting when held.

THAT at said General Meeting, the Society shall elect a

ſtanding Committee, conſiſting of the Preſes, Box-maſters, Clerk, and ſeven other Members, any five to be a *quorum*, to tranſact any buſineſs of the Society that may occur betwixt the ſtated meetings of the Society; theſe proceedings being always ſubject to the review of the next ordinary meeting. And as often as the Committee have occaſion to meet upon the Society's buſineſs, they ſhall be allowed One Shilling and Sixpence out of the Society's Fund, to defray the expence of their meeting. And, at ſaid General Meeting, every Member who is within ten miles of the place of meeting ſhall be obliged to attend, or pay *one ſhilling* and *ſixpence*, to be applied to the general expenditure of the day, except in the caſe of indiſpoſition, which muſt be atteſted by a *Surgeon's* Certificate, and delivered at or previous to the meeting, otherways the excuſe will not be ſuſtained. That beſides the General Meeting there ſhall be three Quarterly Meetings, to be held on the twenty-fifth days of *September*, *December*, and *March*, or *Thurſday* thereafter, at ſeven o'clock in the evening preciſely.

V.

Society's Box how kept; Office-bearers to give security for the Funds; attendance of Office-bearers; attendance of Members at Quarterly Meetings; Fines to increaſe the Stock.

THAT the Society ſhall be provided with a Box for holding the Caſh, Securities, Books, &c. which ſhall have three locks and keys of different conſtructions, to be kept by the Preſes and two Box maſters, who ſhall (if required) give ſecurity for their faithful adminiſtration of the Funds of the Society put into their hands: That the Preſes, Box-maſter, and Clerk, ſhall attend preciſely at the hour of meeting, unless sick or out of town, or forfeit *sixpence;* and if sick or out of town, shall send their key, or forfeit *sixpence;* or if absent the whole night, shall forfeit *one shilling:* That the Officer shall forfeit *one shilling* for every neglect of his duty. And every other Member within three miles of Annan, shall attend all Quarterly Meetings, or send his quarterly payments, or be fined *twopence* for each offence;—the fines to be paid at the first meeting after they are incured, unless a sufficient excuse be offered to the satisfaction of the majority present; and if it can be proven to the satisfaction of the majority, that any who were absent make a false excuse, the fine shall be doubled—All fines to go to the increase of the common Stock.

VI.

Of dissolving the Society, and increasing its Fund; clearing Accounts at the General Meeting.

THAT the Society shall never be dissolved without the consent of five-sixths parts of the Members. And, towards raising a Fund for answering the purposes of the Soceity's institution, every person who is admitted shall pay Ten Shillings and Sixpence of entry-money, and Sixpence for a copy of the Articles; and must produce his Article-book at every General Meeting, or purchase a new one. Also, every Member must pay Two Shillings per quarter, One Shilling and Tenpence to increase the Fund, and Twopence to defray the expence of the meeting. All arrears to be paid up at the June Meeting, or the Member failing to be *excluded:* Provided always, that he shall be allowed to appeal to the next Quarterly Meeting, and if reponed, he shall pay up all arrears, and be fined in *sixpence.*

VII.
Entry-money and Quarterly payments.

THAT the the entry-money is to be paid at the meeting on which the Member is admitted, by his recommender; and the quarterly payment to commence at the firſt General or Quarterly Meeting that ſhall happen thereafter.

VIII.
How money to be lent.

THAT all money (except what may be judged neceſſary by a majority for anſwering the immediate demands on the Society) ſhall be lent or diſpoſed of upon ſuch ſecurity as two-thirds of the Members preſent ſhall direct; and the ſecurity to be taken therefore to be lodged in the Society's Box.

IX.
Allowance to sick Members; when the allowance is reduced.

THAT every Member, after two years entrance; not bringing caſual diſorders on himſelf by raſhneſs or intemperance, whom the LORD ſhall afflict in the courſe of his Providence, ſo as to render him incapable to follow his lawful employment, ſhall be allowed out of the common Stock Six Shillings per week if required, to commence that day week, after proper notice to the Office-bearers, unleſs the diſorder prove of a nature that exceeds thirteen weeks duration,—in which caſe, he ſhall receive Four Shillings per week, which is the leaſt weekly allowance that ſhall be given to any Member, of whatever duration his diſorder may be, except the Funds ſhould at any time be reduced below One Hundred Pounds; in which caſe, every diſtreſſed Member ſhall receive Five Shillings per week for the firft thirteen weeks, and Two Shillings and Sixpence per week during the continuance of his diforder.

X.
Sick visited ; how the allowance is to be given to sick Members in the country ; Members fraudulently obtaining the allowance excluded.

THAT the Prefes and Box-mafter fhall vifit the afflicted Members in Town, and pay them once a-week; and fhall alfo pay the allowance to fick Members in the country once a-week, into the hand of any perfon poffeffed of proper vouchers to receive it, under the penalty of *one shilling* for each neglect, to be paid the firft meeting after conviction; and in order to their judging of the nature and caufe of any Member's indifpofition, they are allowed to confult a *Surgeon* when they think it neceffary, and pay him his charge for advice out of the Society's Funds. And any perfon not within the parifh of Annan, applying for the weekly allowance, muft accompany his application with a Certificate of his indifpofition, by the *Minister* of the parifh where he refides, and the *Surgeon* or *Physician* who attends him ; and if it can be proven that any Member receiving the allowance has not a proper right to it, according to the true intent and meaning of thefe Articles, he fhall be immediately *excluded.*

XI.
Manner of paying funeral charges; ditto of Members wives.

THAT when it fhall pleafe the LORD to remove any Member by death after three years entry, the Society fhall pay Five Pounds towards his funeral; and if a Member's wife die, the Member may receive Two Pounds out of the above fum towards her funeral, by giving a proper receipt for the fame to the Society ; and his heirs are to receive the remaining Three Pounds at his death. Every Member to contribute *sixpence* towards raifing the above fum, at the Member's death, and the deficiency to be made up out of the Funds of the Society. No Member to be allowed to to draw any fum for the burial of more than one wife—The whole to be paid the firft *Monday* after interment.

XII.

Vice-Prefes appointed; how Members are to speak at the Society's meetings, and all irregularities fineable; no Member to leave the room without liberty of the Prefes; and Members refufing to pay the fines excluded.

THAT at every General or Quarterly Meeting the Prefes fhall name a Vice-Prefes, to affift him in keeping order, who fhall have the fame power in that refpect as the Prefes himfelf. And, at every meeting of the Society or Committee, no Member fhall fpeak upon public bufinefs without leave of the Prefes, and muft addrefs his difcourfe to him; and none fhall fpeak but one at a time. And if any Member fhall be drunk at the time of meeting—or curfe, fwear, or behave any-ways indecently or irregularly—or be convicted of faying any thing bad of the Society out of doors—fpreading falfe reports—or expreffing their tranfactions to others unconcerned—rediculing the Prefes or Managers—or cafting up the benefit any Member has received—fuch Member fhall be fined in *fourpence* fterling; and if an Office-bearer, in double that fum : All fuch fines to be impofed by the Prefes, without any vote of the Society, and paid immediately upon conviction. Any Member leaving the club-room before the bufinefs of the meeting is over, without permiffion from the Prefes, fhall forfeit *sixpence*. Any Member refufing to pay fuch fines, fhall be *excluded*.

XIII.

Form of excluding offending Members; Members aggrieved appeal for redress.

THAT the form of excluding offending Members shall be, to dash their names out of the roll at any General or Quarterly Meeting, before the Books are shut, by a voice of a majority of the Members present, on having sufficient evidence of the offence, which shall be recorded in the minutes of the meeting: And if the person so excluded shall think himself aggrieved, it shall be competent for him to appeal to the next General or Quarterly Meeting for redress; but if the sentence be affirmed by the Society at the second meeting, it shall be final to all intents and purposes.

XIV.

Superannuate fund, when commences and how paid, &c.

THAT if any Member live to the age of sixty-four years, he shall be intitled to Five Pounds yearly from the Funds, (over and above the allowance provided for in the former part of these Articles) and to receive the same in two equal portions half-yearly; but no Member to receive the allowance until after fourteen years from the twenty-seventh day of June, one thousand seven hundred and ninety-nine; and no Member to receive said allowance, or superannuated fund, until he has been full twenty-four years a Member, and must then produce a certificate of his age.

XV.

Members receiving the weekly allowance found drinking.

THAT if any Member drawing the weekly allowance according to the preceding Articles, be found or proven to have been drinking, or tippling and drinking in a public house,

particularly at undue hours, his said weekly allowance shall
be withdrawn, and he shall be fined in *five shillings* for said
fault, which, if he refuses to pay, he shall be forthwith *excluded.*

XVI.
Election of a Surgeon, his duty, and fine for neglect.

THAT a Surgeon may be elected annually alongst with the
other Office-bearers, who shall attend all the Members within five miles of Annan, when indisposed, once a-week or
oftener, if found necessary, to give the sick Members his advice, and report their situation to the Office-bearers, or any
one of them; for which he shall be paid One Shilling for
each Member (in the Society) per annum, out of the Funds;
and for each neglect, he shall be fined *one shilling.*

XVII.
Members imposing on the Society excluded.

THAT if it can be proven to the satisfaction of the Society,
that any Member has imposed upon them, by giving himself
up under a false age, in order to attain admission, he shall be
excluded, and his entry-money *forfeited.*

XVIII.
Liquor how ordered, &c.

THAT the Preses and Box masters shall have the sole
power to order in what Liquor they think most proper for the
Society; and no Member shall be allowed to call for any
particular Liquor, without leave of the Preses, under the
penalty of *sixpence* for each offence—which shall be paid
immediately.

XIX.
What Books may be lent out to Members.

THAT the Cafh-Book fhall not be lent out to any Member whatever; but Books that contain regulations for the mangement of the Society, may be lent to a Member, if authorifed by two-thirds of the Members prefent, at any General or Quarterly Meeting—in which cafe, it fhall be returned to the Box-mafter, (in whofe cuftody the Box is lodged) within the courfe of eight days.

XX.
Articles fubject to alterations.

THAT at every General or Quarterly Meeting there can be additions, alterations or amendments, made to all or any of thefe Articles, according to the increafe or decreafe of the Funds; but this not to be competent without the confent of three-fourths of the Members prefent at fuch a meeting.

Form of Application for the Weekly Aliment.

Gentlemen,

I AM not able to follow my lawful employment on account of [*here mention the accident or disorder.*] I therefore apply for the Weekly Allowance of the Society, in terms of the Articles:—This I send as intimation to you. I am,

Gentlemen,

Your humble Servant,

A. B.

To the Preses and Box-masters of the
Trades Society, Annan.

ATTESTATION.

AT ANNAN,

THE SECOND DAY OF JUNE,

one thousand eight hundred and one years.

IN the Quarter Sessions of the Peace for the County of Dumfries, held by adjournment—The RULES and REGU-LATIONS before-written, being exhibited to, and read over by the Justices of the Peace, they unanimously approved of, allow and confirm the same, as being conformable to, and within the meaning of the Act of the 33d year of the reign of his prefent Majesty, made for the encouragement and relief of *Friendly Societies;* and appoint a duplicate of said Rules and Regulations, written upon parchment, to be deposited with the Clerks of the Peace for said County, as directed by the said Act.

(Signed)

JOHN MURRAY, Prefes.

ARTICLES

TO BE OBSERVED BY

THE MEMBERS OF

A

𝕱𝖗𝖎𝖊𝖓𝖉𝖑𝖞 𝕾𝖔𝖈𝖎𝖊𝖙𝖞,

HELD AT THE HOUSE OF

MR. JOHN BAMFORD,

IN

𝕭𝖆𝖗𝖙𝖔𝖓, 𝕹𝖔𝖙𝖙𝖎𝖓𝖌𝖍𝖆𝖒𝖘𝖍𝖎𝖗𝖊.

NOTTINGHAM:

Reprinted by Samuel Tupman, High-Street.

1807.

ARTICLES,

&c. &c.

Imprimis.

THIS Society shall meet on the first Saturday evening in every calendar month, between the hours of six and eight, from Michaelmas to Lady-day, and from Lady-day till Michaelmas, between the hours of seven and nine.

II.

THERE shall be two Stewards belonging to this society; each member shall serve that office in his proper turn, as he stands upon the list, (for half a year) one resigning his office every three months, and his place shall be supplied from off the list as they stand in rotation there; and in like manner shall every steward resign his office when he has served six months.——There shall also be six members called assistants, who shall be taken off the list by turns, preceding the stewards; that is, one every three months, as the eldest of them becomes steward:—they shall, in conjunction with the stewards, visit the sick, and collect the payments, if required; and every member that shall refuse to serve these offices in his proper turn, shall forfeit and pay *two shillings and sixpence.*——The money that is already raised or hereafter shall be raiſed by theſe preſents, ſhall be paid and applied by the ſtewards, to ſuch uſes as the following rules and orders direct and appoint.

III.

EVERY member ſhall, upon the firſt Saturday evening in every calendar month, pay to the ſtew-ards for the time being, the ſum of *one shilling*, out of which they ſhall expend the ſum of *two pence ;* and as a penalty for every neglect in the ſaid pay-ments, each member ſhall forfeit and pay for the firſt default *two pence*, for the ſecond *four pence*, and for the third ſhall be totally excluded the ſociety.

IV.

THAT every perſon who ſhall be admitted a member of this ſociety, ſhall, at his ſigning and ſealing theſe preſents, pay the ſum of ~~six shillings~~ entrance. ~~and one year's monthly payments into the stock, or otherwise~~ he ſhall pay *one shilling* entrance, and two year's monthly payments, before he ſhall be entitled to any benefit from the ſtock : and when he hath made good his payments and forfeitures for the time above mentioned, he ſhall receive the benefit as is hereafter directed in the ſucceeding Articles.

V.

THE money that is already raiſed by theſe pre-ſents being put out to intereſt, the notes thereof being put into the hands of Mr. Richard Steven-ſon, Mr. John Wallis, and Mr. John Stevenſon, whom we have appointed Treaſurers of this ſociety.

VI.

THE money that we have in hand, and hereafter

may have, fhall be kept in a box, and depofited in
the hands of the mafter or miftrefs of the houfe
where the fociety is kept, they giving fecurity for
the fafety of the fame, until fuch time as the ftewards fhall think proper to put it out to intereft;
and the fecurity they fhall give for it fhall be put
into the hands of fome one of the Treafurers.

VII.

For the better collecting the faid payments, the
two ftewards fhall meet on the firft Saturday in
every calendar month as aforefaid, in the fociety-
room at the hours appointed, and fhall there continue the fpace of two hours, to receive all fuch
money as fhall be brought or fent by the members
of this fociety: and every fteward not coming or
fending his key by the hours appointed, fhall forfeit
one shilling; and every fteward that fhall be abfent
when the time of two hours is expired, fhall forfeit
and pay *six pence*, unlefs he procures fome other
member to act in his ftead.

VIII.

The ftewards fhall have power to command
filence at all meetings, and every member who
doth not obey this command at the third time of
its being repeated, fhall forfeit and pay *two-pence*.

IX.

If any member comes to the fociety difguifed
in liquor, he fhall forfeit and pay *six-pence;* if any
curfe or fwear, or offers to lay any wager, or give
any member the lie, or infult any one in any cafe
whatfoever, he or they fhall forfeit and pay *two-
pence* for every fuch offence: and if any member

ftrikes another, at any time of meeting, he fhall forfeit *one shilling*.

X.

There is a Clerk belonging to this fociety, who doth attend each meeting at the time appointed for the ftewards, or forfeit *one shilling*, unlefs he procures fome other member to act in his ftead; and he continues there whilft the ftewards ftay upon bufinefs. He keeps the accounts belonging to the fociety; for which fervice he only pays *two-pence* every five weeks, and *four-pence* every four week's meeting: he is then entitled to the benefit the fame as the reft of the members;—and he receives *two-pence* of every frefh member that enters into this fociety.

XI.

No perfon will be admitted a member of this fociety who lives more than four miles from Barton; yet if any member, for the better maintenance of himfelf and family, or on any other lawful occafion, fhall remove more than four miles from Barton aforefaid, and fhall fall fick or lame, &c. fo as to be incapable of doing any manner of bufinefs, he may fend a certificate, figned by the minifter and churchwardens of the parifh where he refides, to one of the ftewards, or to the mafter of the houfe where the fociety is held, teftifying his inability to work; and at one week's end after date, or two weeks, &c. figned as above, authorifing fome proper perfon to receive his money, who fhall give a receipt for the fame: for neither ftewards or affiftants fhall be obliged to vifit any member more than four miles from Barton.—And if any member impofe on the fociety in this or any other article, he fhall be excluded this fociety for ever.

XII.

It is agreed by this fociety, that no perfon fhall become a member thereof who hath not had that fore complaint called the fmallpox; and if any perfon fhall fo offer himfelf, and be entered, it not being known, he fhall not receive any benefit from the box, providing he fhall have that diforder afterwards, nor for any diforder they may leave upon him.

XIII.

The members of this fociety may extend to any number that the majority fhall think proper.

XIV.

No perfon will be admitted a member of this fociety who is above the age of thirty years, unlefs by the unanimous confent of the members.

XV.

If any member of this fociety fhall difclofe any fecret relating thereto; that is, who voted for or againft any one, or what arguments were made ufe of, for or againft him, fo as to make any difpute or difturbance, he fhall, on due proof thereof, forfeit the fum of *one shilling* for every fuch offence.

XVI.

It is agreed by the members of this fociety, that every perfon, a member thereof, fhall pay, or caufe to be paid, on the firft Saturday evening in January and July, all his payments and forfeitures whatfoever, and of what nature and kind foever, that is juftly and fairly adjudged lawful by the majority of this fociety. But in cafe of non-payment on

the above-mentioned evenings, he fhall be allowed
until the next club-night following, which is in
February and Auguſt, providing he doth forfeit
and pay *one shilling* over and above all his other
payments and forfeitures; if not, he fhall be excluded this fociety.

XVII.

Iт is alfo agreed by this fociety, that it fhall not
be diffolved, or broke up, upon any confideration
whatfoever, whilſt there remains three of the members to continue and carry it on : and whofoever
of the faid members voluntarily declares off and
leaves the fociety, fhall not be entitled to draw any
money out of the ſtock.

XVIII.

Tнıs fociety fhall not be removed to any other
houfe without a juſt caufe, of which the majority
are to be allowed proper judges.

XIX.

Proper Books fhall be kept for the ufe of the
fociety, for the clerk to keep accounts in.

XX.

Tнат every perfon who now is, or hereafter
may be admitted a member of this fociety, having
made good his payments as before mentioned, for
the fpace of one whole year, or two whole years,
as is expreffed in the fourth article, fhall fall fick,
lame, blind, or otherwife unable to work for his
livelihood, fhall weekly receive out of the ſtock
the fum of ~~five~~ *shillings*, for half a year, provided
his illnefs or inability to work continues fo long,
and after that time only *three shillings* per week,

for the time that his illness or inability to work continues.

XXI.

IF any member at his falling sick or lame, &c. owe to the box any payments or forfeitures whatsoever, the stewards shall have power to stop it out of his first week's payment, if he thinks it necessary.

XXII.

AFTER proper notice is given to the stewards of a member's being sick or lame, &c. the stewards and assistants shall visit all such members once every week, two at one time and two at another, by turns, within the limits above-mentioned; and for neglect of such visits, they shall forfeit *one shilling* each: that is, the stewards and assistants at every three months' end, when one of them goes out of office, shall settle which of them shall visit together for the next three months following, when there is occasion, and have it wrote down on a piece of paper, that there may be no mistake in the account; and when it shall happen to be five weeks between club-nights, the two stewards for the time being shall attend the fifth week over and above. And the sick or lame person shall write, or cause to be wrote, a certificate of the stewards' and assistants' names, and day of the month of every one who comes to visit him; which account he shall either deliver in himself, or send it to the society on each club-night after the time of his receiving money from the box: and if such person either refuse or neglect to give or send such account at the time mentioned, he shall forfeit and pay *one shilling.*————And if either steward or

B

affiftant fhould happen to be fick or lame, &c.
themfelves, they fhould nominate fome other member to act in their ftead: and if fuch member fo
nominated fhall refufe to act, he fhall forfeit and
pay *six pence.*

XXIII.

Wʜᴇɴ Providence fhall pleafe to deprive us of
a member of this fociety by death, the clerk, two
ftewards, and three others they fhall nominate,
fhall meet at fome convenient place that they fhall
appoint, (and take with them the pall, hatbands,
and other articles provided for fuch ufes,) from
whence they fhall go to the place where the deceafed member is, and attend his corpfe to the
grave; and the fix members that attend fhall be
allowed *one shilling and six-pence* each, out of
the box, to bear their expences.

XXIV.

Iᴛ is alfo agreed, that every member of this fociety fhall be entitled to the pall belonging thereto
for the ufe of his wife's funeral; and if it be let
out for the ufe of any other perfon, they fhall pay
one shilling and six pence for the ufe of it.

XXV.

Iғ it pleafe God to deprive any member of this
fociety of his wife by death, if he chufes he may
receive *one guinea* from the box, or let it lie until
his own deceafe.

XXVI.

Tʜᴀᴛ at the death of every member of this fociety, who hath made good all his payments and
forfeitures whatf ever, for one whole year, or two
whole years, as mentioned in the preceding articles,

—his widow, or executor, or whom he fhall appoint, fhall immediately, or as foon as the ftewards can conveniently meet, receive out of the faid ftock, the fum of *two pounds* to bury him, and on the next club-night after, *thirty shillings* more, and then fhall be excluded any further benefit or advantage.

XXVII.

I f any member who hath not been entered one year, or two years as before mentioned, fhall die, his widow, or executor, &c. fhall receive back all fuch fums as the deceafed hath paid into the ftock, if nothing is wanting of all his payments and forfeitures relating thereto.

XXVIII.

I f any member feigns himfelf fick or lame, or takes himfelf off the club when fick or lame, &c. with an intent of defrauding the fociety, and it is proved againft him, he fhall for ever be excluded therefrom.

XXIX.

I t is alfo agreed, that if any perfon come to be admitted into this fociety, he fhall go into fome other room whilft the fociety debate, if any objection is made againft him.

XXX.

A Feast fhall be kept every Whitfun-Monday at the fociety's room : every member fhall pay *one shilling* towards the expence of that day; the reft of the expences to be paid out of the box.—Each member hereof fhall receive one blue ribband for the firft time; and afterwards if he does not appear at that time in a decent one, fuch as fhall be approved off by the ftewards and affiftants, he or they fhall forfeit *one shilling*.

XXXI.

EVERY member fhall meet at the club-room on the feaft-day, to go to church; and if he be not there to anfwer to his name at going to church, he fhall forfeit *two shillings and six-pence*, unlefs detained by illnefs.——If any member refufe to be conformable to rules and orders already prefcribed, as at other meetings, fhall forfeit *one shilling*.

XXXI.

It is alfo univerfally agreed by this fociety, that if through cafualties or misfortunes the ftock fhall be reduced below the fum of *thirty pounds*, every member thereof fhall pay *two-pence* per week over and above his other payments and forfeitures, until fuch time as the ftock fhall be increafed to above the faid fum of *thirty pounds* again.

XXXIII.

IF any perfon before or at the time of his admittance, labour under any infirmity or difeafe whatfoever, and fhall afterwards be ill or lame of fuch infirmity, he fhall receive no benefit from the ftock, provided he concealed fuch infirmity, &c. at the time of his admittance.

XXXIV.

ALL forfeits whatfoever relating to thefe articles fhall go into the box.

XXXV.

THERE fhall be a general meeting of every member, on the firft Saturday evening in January and July ; and every member that does not appear on thofe nights, fhall forfeit, over and above all other forfeitures, the fum of *two-pence.*

XXXVI.

THAT if any member fhall have the venereal difeafe, or fhall fall fick or lame occafioned by any unlawful exercife whatever,—as wreftling, fighting, boxing, jumping, &c. or through excefs of drinking, he fhall receive no benefit from the box.

XXXVII.

ALL controverfies that may arife at any time relating to this fociety, that cannot be decided by the articles, fhall be ordered by a majority of the members then prefent.

XXXVIII.

IF the ftewards and affiftants fhall fuffer more drink to be brought into the club-room (during the limited two hours) than each man's quota of *two-pence,* they fhall pay for it themfelves.

XXXIX.

IF there be an extraordinary occafion to fummon the members to do any occafional bufinefs, every member who does not attend that hath an order from the ftewards, fhall forfeit *six pence,* and the ftewards fhall expend the fum of *five shillings* out of the ftock, at that meeting, on the members that attend it. But if the ftewards fhall call any fuch meeting unlaw u y, they fhall pay the expence themfelves, or be excluded.

XL.

THE ftewards and affiftants themfelves fhall be fubject to all thefe rules and orders which are contained herein, and enforce them upon the reft of the members (when adjudged lawful,) without any partiality or refpeϵt of perfons : and the ftewards or affiftants who fhall negleϵt to do their duty in thefe refpeϵts, fhall forfeit the fum of *six pence*.

XLI.

LASTLY,—That peace and quietnefs may continue in this Friendly Society, we have mutually agreed,—that if any member hereof fhall offer any abufe, or make any difturbance concerning any thing that fhall be lawfully done according to thefe articles, he fhall pay for the firft default *sixpence* ; for the fecond *one shilling :* and for the third fhall be totally excluded from this fociety.

NOTTINGHAMSHIRE.————At the General Quarter-Sessions of the Peace of our Sovereign Lord the KING, holden at the Shire Hall in Nottingham, in and for the said County, the twenty-eighth day of April, in the year of our Lord 1794,—before Thomas Charlton, William Milnes, William Sherbrooke, and William Watson, Esquires, and also William Becher, William Thompson, James Bingham, John Walter, and Charles Wylde, Clerk, Justice of our said Lord the King, assigned to keep the Peace in the said County; the above Rules, Orders, and Regulations, were confirmed by the Justices there assembled, pursuant to the directions of the statute made in the thirty-third year of the reign of his present Majesty, intituled " an Act for the Encouragement and Relief of Friendly Societies."

JOB. BROUGH, Clerk of the Peace.

———

GEORGE HOLMES, Clerk.

THOMAS RICE, } Stewards.
SAMUEL BROWN, }

ISAAC PRIESTLEY, ⎫
RICH. WILKINSGN, ⎪
JOHN OLIVER, ⎬ Assistants.
WILLIAM ALSOP, ⎪
JOHN SMITH, ⎪
GEORGE SMITH. ⎭

———

NOTTINGHAM:

Reprinted by Samuel Tupman, High-Street.

1807.

ORDERS

TO BE OBSERVED BY A

SOCIETY OF TAYLORS,

HELD AT THE HOUSE OF

MR. PETER MARSHALL,

THE

ALPHABET, Stanhope Street, Clare Market,

LONDON:

BEGAN DECEMBER 31, 1787.

---

*FORASMUCH as it hath been an antient custom in this
our Kingdom of England, for divers Artists to meet
together and unite themselves; but more especially for
those who practice this our Art and Mystery of a Taylor,
and in true Christian Charity, upon just Occasions, to
assist each other: We therefore of this Society, have
mutually agreed to these present Articles, as followeth.*

NATHANIEL ALDERSON,
WILLIAM SMITH,
DANIEL BEASLEY,
CHARLES ATKINSON,
} STEWARDS.

JAMES MANN, CLERK, No. 3, *Bury Street, Bloomsbury.*

LONDON:

PRINTED BY G. SMEETON, 17, ST. MARTIN'S LANE.

1809.

A TABLE,

Shewing the Day of the Month of each Meeting Night, for Ten Years to come, which may be understood by the following Rules, viz. Look for the Date of the Year on the Side of the Table, and then look up the Month, and you will find the Day the Meeting Night is of.

Those marked thus * are Grace Nights.

	1818	1817	1816	1815	181?	1813	1812	1812	1810	180?
Jan.	8*	5*	3*	*	6*	7*	9*	9*	9*	2
Feb.	4	1 11	7 14	9 16	10 17	1 18	13 20	13 20	13 20	6 1?
'rch	26	29	28	23	31		26	27	27	27
pril	1*	*	4*	8*	7	8*	2*	3	3	3
May	13 20*	8 15*	11 18*	6 23*	12 19*	13 20*	7 14*	8 15*	8 15*	8 15*
'ine	31	23	27	28	30			26	26	26
uly	7	30*	2*	5*	7*	8*	9*	3*	3*	2*
August	2 9*	6 13*	8 15*	9 16*	11 18*	13 19*	13 20*	7 14*	7 14*	7 14*
eptr.		30		28		30				
Oct.	4 11*	2 9	5 12*		6 13	7	1 8*	2 9	2 9	2 9
Nov.	5 12	7 14*	6 13	3 16	7 21*	1 18	2 19	13 20	13 20	3 20
'ec.	29		26	21	3	3				

ORDERS, &c.

ARTICLE 1.

THERE shall be a meeting of this society, **twice in** every quarter of a year, that is to say upon the first Monday after every quarter day, and also upon every sixth Monday following, at the house where the club is kept, at eight o'clock in the evening, and continue 'till ten o'clock; likewise a box shall be provid d wi h five locks, and five keys, the man or woman of the house to keep one, and the stewards one key each, the charge thereof to be paid out of the box, and none shall be admitted into this society but Taylors, and of no other country than England, Wales, and Scotland, and no person can be admitted a member without the consent of this society.

II. Every person that enters into this society, shall pay 5s. and 3d. for entrance and articles, and every club night shall pay 2s. 6d. into the box, and 3d. to the house for beer; and no person can be admitted into this society that is above 34 years of age.

III. The members of this society shall serve the office of steward by their seniority in the book, and notice shall be given by the clerk, six weeks before the time, in the club room before ten o'clock, and whosoever shall refuse to stand on the half yearly night, shall pay 5s. to the box, or be excluded this society; and when so chosen, to serve half a year, no member to serve as steward till he is free of this society.

IV. No

IV. No person entering into this society can receive any benefit, 'till he has been in the same nine months, that is to say six half quarters, but after that time, if he is rendered incapable of working, he shall receive 15s. per week during his illness, but if the interest of the stock amount to 21l. per annum or more, then the sick member or members shall receive 17s. and pensioners 5s. per week; and if his disorder require his removing into the country, and with the advice of a doctor to regain his health, the stewards shall make provision accordingly, not exceeding one months pay. No sick member to go in the country without two or more of the stewards seeing him.

V. No person shall receive any benefit from the stock of this society that had any distemper prior to his entrance, or whose sickness, lameness or blindness, shall be caused by fighting or quarrelling, except in his own defence, or by being in any riot or drunkeness, or the veneral disease; any members illness being proved to be occasioned by any of the above mentioned causes, while he receives or claims any benefit of this society, and the same be proved by any one or more members, upon oath taken before a magistrate, he shall be excluded, except he can clearly prove to the society that he did not know his disorder proceeded from any of the above complaints; but if the same should terminate in his death, his friends shall receive the same benefit as specified at the death of any other free member, in case he has not declared on the box with any of the aforesaid complaints.

VI. That if any member by Divine Providence, shall through age or affliction become blind or lame, and thereby rendered incapable of working, he shall while living receive 4s. per week, and be excused all payments whatsoever; but if ever he is capable of earning 1l. 1s. per week at his trade, or any other way, his pension shall be taken off, and shall be admitted a member as before.

VII. If

VII. If any member is taken ill, he shall have the allowance of this society for 9 months, and then if there is no likelihood of his recovering his health, he shall be put on the pension; but if it appears he cannot long survive, h. shall have the usual allowance of 15s. or 17s. per week; but if any man declare off to avoid the pension, and it is clearly proved to the society, he or they shall have their payment stopped for three months.

VIII. The clerk and stewards of this society, shall attend every club night by 8 o'clock, and likewise the Monday following, or for such neglect shall forfeit 1s. to the box, but if not there by 9 o'clock, shall forfeit 2s. to the box, and pay all expences for forcing open the box, if required; and if one of the stewards do not visit the sick, within twenty four hours after notice given him, he shall forfeit 2s. 6d. to the box, and the landlord shall give notice to one of the stewards, within twenty four hours af er the sick man has declared on the box, or be fined 2s. 6d. and no member can receive any benefit 'till the eighth day of his declaring on the box, the day he declares on ot being reckoned as one; and if he is found at work, or any kind of gaming while he is on the box, he shall be excluded.

IX. If any member of this society goes into the country and be there visited with sickness, he must send his letters to the landlord of the house, where the club is kept, signed by the Minister and Church-wardens, or Overseers of the parish where he resides, once every month, during his sickness, or else he can receive no benefit from the society, and no person shall receive any benefit that does not reside in either England, Wales, or Scotland

X. The stewards shall receive and pay all, and at the end of their time, give and deliver up a particular account of their proceedings, together with their receipts and disbursements, who shall appoint a committee to audit the same to the society, and the succeeding stewards shall give their address to the landlord of the house, that the member

may

may be visited when he is sick; and each steward shall visit the sick at least once every week, (each on different days,) to see the society is not injured; but if he neglect to visit any member, after notice given him, he or they shall forfeit 2s. 6d. for each neglect.

XI. If any member absents himself, and doth not send his quarterly contribution, at the end of three half quarters, by eleven o'clock at night, he shall be excluded; and for the better support of this society, each member at the end of every half year shall pay one shilling into the box, over and above his quarterly payments; and at the same time shall pay all that he is in arrears to the box, or be excluded; any member being so excluded, shall receive notice of what fines are due on the box, before the next grace night, at which time if he clears the book, and pays the fine of 2s. 6d. he shall be replaced as before. No member so excluded can receive any benefit till he is re-entered.

XII. Every person when admitted a member of this society, shall give in his name, age, and place of abode, to be registered by the clerk, and in case of removal, shall inform the clerk on the next club night after, or forfeit 1s. to the box.

XIII. That the clerk do give or send a summons to every member that is fined for steward; likewise send a summons for all other payments between the club and grace night, if not ordered by the members that attend on the club night, to be marked present; if he neglect so to do he shall pay the fine of 2s. 6d. to the box.

XIV. If any dispute shall arise relating to this society, it shall be determined by the majority of the members then present; but if the members think proper to alter any of the articles, then the steward shall give public notice, and if required by the majority then present, the clerk shall send a summons to the rest of the members, to attend on the next club night; each one neglecting to attend, to forfeit 6d. to the box; each Member to pay 2d. to the
clerk

clerk for his summons, on all occasions. No member to come under this article that resides out of the bills of mortality, except those who reside in Mary-le-bone, or St. Pancras.

XV. If any member of this society shall be impressed into his Majesty's service, by sea or land, and shall be lame or rendered incapable to work, he shall receive the benefit of this society, if his payments are kept up, but if he enter voluntarily into his Majesty's service, he shall be excluded.

XVI. If any member dies abroad, he shall be allowed 4l. for funeral expences, (if the parties bring a proper certificate of his death,) with 10l. as a legacy; both to be paid the first club night after the death of the member, to the nearest relation or friend, whom the deceased shall have bequeathed it to; but if the stewards think the person that claims it has no right to it, the money shall remain in the box, till the third half quarter after the death, or untill there shall be satisfactory proof of heirship or bequest.

XVII. If any member shall curse or swear in club hours, he shall forfeit 2d. for every oath or curse; and if any member lays wagers, or lessens a brother member, in regard to his trade, or comes into the club room disguised in liquor, or refuse to keep silence, after the stewards have called silence three different times, shall forfeit 6d. for each offence.

VIII. At the decease of any member, there shall be notice given by the clerk or stewards, on the first club night after the decease, in the club room, that all the members may be acquainted therewith.

XIX. If any member shall call for liquor without the stewards leave, he shall pay for it himself, exclusive of his club money, and if the stewards call for more than each man's club money, they shall pay the overplus out of their own pockets.

XX. If any member shall privately promote the breaking up of this society, and inform any other member of it, and
he

he conceals the same, if afterwards notice is given to the society, then he or they shall e excluded.

XXI. If the stewards shal embezzle any part of the stock they are entrusted with, for the payment of the sick, he or hey so offending shall be excluded, and be prosecuted for the fraud.

XXII. That no sum or sums of money shall be lent to any person out of the stock of this socie y; but on lawful interest, nd good security, such as shall be approved of by the society, and 10s. 6d. shall be allowed to such as shall go to put out any money, or take out any money, and 5s. to those that goes to receive the interest; no one shall be a stock holder any longer than he is a member of this society, and resident within the bills of mortality, and if a stock holder dies, the stock he held shall be transferred into another member's name, before the legacy due to the claimants are paid.

XXIII. It is agreed, that at the death of any free member, there shall b a coffin, pall and shroud provided, not exceeding four pounds, and the stewards shall see such member decently interred, at the charge of the society, in any burial ground the deceased or his friends may appoint, any friend of the deceased may have 4l. for the funeral expences, and then the stewards shall be excused from their attendance, and 10l. as a legacy as before mentioned.

XXIV. No person shall serve as clerk of this society, unless he is a member of the same, and he shall be excused all payments whatsoever, and receive 10s. 6d. per quarter, and receive the benefit from the box whenever his necessity requires it; and this society shall not be removed from the house where it is now kept, but on a just occasion.

XXV. A free member may have the liberty of drawing 4l. from the stock on the death of his wife, and give a stamp receipt for the same, which receipt, shall on the death of such a member be paid to his representatives as 4l. of his legacy. Members claiming the benefit of this article, must
bring

bring a proper certificate of their marriage, or make affidavit of the same, and not to be allowed for more than one wife.

XXVI. The stewards are to attend the house every Monday night, between 8 and 9 o'clock at night, in order to hear a y complaints that may be made respecting the sick, and also to settle among themselves concerning any new declaration, on or off t e box, or forfeit 6d. each one absent, these sixpences to be spent by those that do attend. Any member refusing to pay the above fine on the following club or grace night shall be excluded.

XXVII. It is agreed by this society, if any member of it is on the box, and shall quit his lodgings without leaving word where the stewards may see him, he or they shall forfeit 2s. 6d. to the box, but if out of his lodgings after 9 o'clock at night, he shall be deprived of one weeks allowance; for the second offence two weeks, and for the third shall be excluded.

XXVIII. It is agreed by this society, that members, may be entered on a grace night, but should there be any objection, and a majority should consider it as a relevant one, on the club night following, the man so entered to have his money returned him.

XXIX. That if any member or members of this society, shall give trouble to the steward or stewards, or to any other member, or clerk, for acting or doing any thing strictly according to these rules, orders, and regulations, they shall be re-embursed all lawful charges, that he or they may be at in defending themselves against their adversaries, out of the box, and if any member, steward, or clerk shall be called on any extraordinary business in the service of this society, he or they shall be paid all reasonable expences for his trouble and lost time.

XXX. That in order to preserve as much as possible, the harmony of this society, it is agreed, that in case any dispute should arise between any members of this society, that all such disputes shall be settled by arbitration, and
the

the said arbitrators to be nominated by each of the respective parties, as the act directs; the decision of the
arbitrators sh.ll be binding, final and conclusive on all
parties, to all intents and purposes, without appeal or being
subject to the controul of two or more justices of peace,
agreeably to the said act in that case made and provided;
and that when any member or members of this society, shall
find himself or themselves agrieved, and the general opinion
of the society on the case is not satisfactory to the party
complaining, it shall be lawful for such person or persons
to chuse three free members, and for the society to chuse
three free members alternately, and those six rbitrators,
or a majority of them, shall appoint a president from the
members of the society, to meet at such time and place as
shall be agreed upon by the parties, to consider the matter
in dispute, and whatever award, order, or determination,
shall be made by the said arbitrators, or a majority of them,
shall be final and decisive. But if it should so happen, that
an equal number of the said arbitrators maintain a different
opinion, it shall be submitted to the decision of the president appointed thereunto, and from whose decision there
shall be no appeal, and all reasonable expences attending
arbitrations shall be paid for from the stock, and if any
member shall knowingly and wrongfully accuse another, he
or they shall be fined 5s each, or in default of payment of
the said fine he shall be excluded.

FINIS.

A T the General Quarter Sessions of the Peace, of our Lord the King, holden at the Guildhall in the Sanctuary, Westminster, in and for the City and Liberty of Westminster, on Wednesday the 5th Day of April, in the Forty-ninth Year of the Reign of our Sovereign Lord George the Third, King of Great Britain, &c. Before William Mainwaring, Charles Churchill, Hugh Dive, Patrick Colquhoun, Esquires, and others their fellow Justices of our said Lord the King, assigned to keep the Peace in the Liberty aforesaid. And also to hear and determine divers Felonies, Trespasses, and other Misdemeanors committed in the same Liberty——

The several Rules, Orders, and Regulations (before mentioned) are by the Justices, now here, after due examination thereof, allowed and confirmed, pursuant to the Statute in such case made and provided.

By the Court,

VAUGHAN.

C. Smeeton, Printer, 17, St. Martin's Lane, London.

ARTICLES

AND

REGULATIONS

FOR

GOVERNING

THE

TOWN PORTERS'
FRIENDLY SOCIETY,

INSTITUTED 12TH MARCH 1688;

AND REVISED AND AMENDED 8TH MARCH 1833.

To aid each other in distress ;
To make the wants of old age less ;
Or should a Member die ;
His new-made Widow to assist,
To lay his body in the dust ;
These are the objects, surely just,
Of our Society.

EDINBURGH :
PRINTED BY JOHN M'DONALD,
13, CARRUBBERS' CLOSE.

MDCCCXXXIII.

CONTENTS.

PENALTIES.

ARTICLES, &c.

INTRODUCTION.

As the importance of Friendly Societies is of great benefit to the labouring classes, they are to be found in every part of the kingdom. With a view to prevent, as far as possible, any person who may join this Society from being reduced to want, or being burdensome to the public, in the time of sickness, lameness, or any other disease which Providence may be pleased to visit them with during life, a few well-disposed persons, along with the Bailies of Edinburgh, did, on the 12th of March 1688, form themselves into a Friendly Society, by the name of " The Town Porters' Friendly Society;" and now, finding their former Laws and Articles incomplete, it was found, from the experience of the Members, requisite, for the good of said Society, to make such alterations as their business from a series of years necessarily required, in order that their minutes of sederunts might correspond therewith, and also to avoid mistakes. They therefore declare, that they determine to stand by the subsequent Articles, as the rules of this Society, from and after this date, and to such minutes as the Society shall judge proper to be adopted from time to time, all which shall be equally binding as the following Articles, when sanctioned in terms of the Act of the 10th Geo. IV. cap. 56.

OBJECT OF THE INSTITUTION, AND PLACE OF MEETING.

Art. I. The Society shall be named THE TOWN PORTERS' FRIENDLY SOCIETY; and its object is, with a view to prevent, as far as possible, any person who may join it from being reduced to want either from sickness or lameness, provided that he is not the cause of bringing his trouble on himself by intemperance or any other bad conduct, in the manner after-mentioned, viz.—*First,* For affording a weekly payment in money to the Members of the Society during sickness, lameness, or inability to attend to their usual employment, provided such sickness, lameness, or inability be not continued longer than hereafter-mentioned; and, *Second,* For affording a sum, payable at the death of the Members, and their Wives or Widows, towards defraying the expenses of their funeral, and for gathering in our several proportions of money, managing, improving, and disposing of our Stock and Funds for our joint use and behoof, as hereafter-directed, to which declared purposes of the Society, the whole Funds shall be exclusively applied.

All the Meetings of the Society shall be held in Stevenson's Room, Advocates' Close, High Street, City of Edinburgh. If changed, intimation will be given in due time, according to the provisions of the Act of Parliament.

QUALIFICATIONS NECESSARY FOR ENTRANTS.

II. That persons of different callings and employments may be admitted, who shall be recommended by two of the Members, to be of a sound and healthy constitution, free of maim, bruise, hereditary or constitutional disease, capable to gain an honest livelihood by their employment, of a good moral character, and his wife, if he has one, in good health. At the time when any person is proposed for entry as a Member of this Society, he must answer all the above questions to the satisfaction of the present Members, who may reject or admit him, as they may think proper, without assigning their reasons for so doing. If any person is admitted a Member, and the Society procuring information, before he has paid two quarter-accounts into the Funds, that he is an improper Member, his name shall be struck off the roll, and what money he has paid returned to him, without the Society being obliged to assign any reason for so doing; and each entrant shall subscribe an adherence to these regulations.

ENTRY AND AGES.

III. Every entrant shall pay the sum of one pound ten shillings sterling of entry-money, the price of a copy of the articles, one shilling to the Clerk, and a sixpence to the officer, as their fees, before receiving a line for his badge; and every entrant shall produce an extract of his age, or such other testimony, as may be satisfactory to the Society at entering, or at the first quarter-day after; and if any person impose on the Society by underrating his age one or two years at entering, he shall pay double the entry-money for underrating his age, and if, after it is proven against him, that he has underrated his age, he persists to defraud the Society, he shall forfeit all he has paid, and be no longer a Member. No person shall be admitted a Member of this Society who is above thirty-six years of age at the time of his application for admission; and persons being under twenty-one years of age shall only be admitted with consent of their parents, master, or guardians.

ENTRANTS NOT ENTITLED TO SICK-MONEY.

IV. No Member shall be entitled to Sick-money or Funeral-allowance, or any part thereof, until he is a full year and six months a Member, from the date of his entry, and till he has cleared all arrears on the books; but should a Member die before the expiration of that time, all the payments made by him shall be returned to his widow, or other legal representative, with the exception of his entry, fines, and Clerk and Officer's fees; and the widow shall have no more claim on the Society. And all Members dying, before receiving the allowance for his interment, must deliver up the deceased Member's badge to the Treasurer of the Society; and any Member who may give up his badge, while in life, shall have no more claim on the Society thereafter.

ENTRANTS IMPOSING ON THE SOCIETY.

V. If it shall at any time be proven that a Member has imposed on the Society at entry, by underrating his age for one or more years, or by producing a false certificate, or other false evidence of his age, or by misrepresenting his own or his wife's health, or concealing any complaint which may tend to prevent him from following his usual employment, such Member shall be expelled the Society, and shall forfeit all the money he has contributed; also, any Member or Members recommending any individual, knowing him to be disqualified as above, shall each be liable to a fine of Five Shillings sterling for their misdemeanour.

STATUTORY MEETINGS.

VI. The Society shall have four Quarterly Meetings, viz.—Upon the second Thursday of November, February, May, and August, the first of which shall be the head quarter-day, for electing office-bearers for the ensuing year, and for settling all the transactions, and balancing the books of the bygone year; and, for convenience to the Members, a Committee Meeting shall be held the first Friday after each quarter-day, for taking in arrears, balancing the books and cash transactions of the bygone quarter.

ORDER OF BUSINESS ON QUARTER-NIGHTS.

VII. At a quarter of an hour after the specified time of meeting, the Clerk shall call the roll of Committee, mark those who are absent, after which he shall proceed to call the roll of the Society, when each Member shall, at the calling of his name, pay his quarter-account, or whatever sum he may be due the Society; the Clerk shall then proceed to call the roll a second time, to receive the money from those Members who were not present at the calling of the first roll; and no money is to be taken, nor partial payments to be received, at any time after the books shall have been open for two hours ; and no money shall be taken from Members in arrears between quarter-days, as all arrears must be paid on the quarter or eight-day Meetings, and clear on the books, to entitle them to the benefit of the Funds of the Society. When the money is all collected, it shall be paid over to the Treasurer, after which any other business relating to the Society may be introduced, but no discussion of other matters during the time of collecting the money.

BEHAVIOUR AT MEETINGS.

VIII. Members speaking in the Society must do so by addressing the Preses standing and uncovered, and in direct reference to the question or business before the Society ; and if any Member come to any Meeting intoxicated with liquor, and behave disorderly while there, by applying improper language, or speak to any Member in a rude and unbecoming manner, he shall be called to order by the Preses, and be fined for the first transgression Sixpence, and if he repeats the offence on the same night, One Shilling for the second offence, and so on for every transgression ; and if he continues disorderly, he must leave the Meeting, and be fined as the Act directs ; and if he still continues obstinate, he shall be expelled from any benefit until he pay his fine, and acknowledge his fault. All fines shall go to the Funds of the Society.

EXTRAORDINARY MEETINGS.

IX. If at any time it is found necessary to call an Extraordinary Meeting of the Society, the roll shall be called at a quarter of an hour after the time specified for the meeting ; and every Member absent after the second roll is called, who were absentees at the first roll-call, shall, if duly warned, pay a fine of Sixpence, unless a satisfactory excuse is made to the Society ; and any of the office-bearers who are absent shall pay the same fine as when absent at a Quarter or Committee Meeting. If any Member shall leave any Meeting without permission being asked and granted by the Preses, he shall be fined Threepence. Every Member in health, residing within the bounds of warning, if absent when the roll is called for the election of office-bearers, shall pay a fine of One Shilling sterling, and no excuse except personal or family distress.

OFFICE-BEARERS.

X. The Society shall always be under the direction of a Preses, Old Preses, Treasurer, Constable, and three Key-masters, who must be free Members, and twelve Assistants, who, together, shall form a Standing Committee for managing the affairs of the Society ; but all their transactions shall be liable to the inspection and control of the Society at large, at each next ensuing meeting thereof; and the whole shall be chosen annually from among the Members of the Society. The transactions of the Standing Committee shall be regularly entered in a Minute-book.

ELECTION OF OFFICE-BEARERS.

XI. And be it enacted, that upon the second Thursday of November annually, being the head quarter-day, there shall be a poll election for a Preses, and Treasurer, and three Key-masters. The roll shall be called, 1*st*, To nominate candidates; the three highest in votes shall retire, and out of these three a Preses shall be chosen by a majority of votes; a Treasurer shall be chosen in the same manner; one calling of the roll for the Key-masters. Should the Preses, Treasurer, or Key-masters refuse to serve, the next highest in votes shall be considered duly elected; and should they likewise refuse to serve, in such case another election shall take place in the same manner before-mentioned. The Preses last in office shall always sit as a Committee Member, and officiate as Preses, if necessary. The twelve Assistants or Committee Members shall be taken from the roll by rotation, and if any Member is not present when it comes to his name by rotation, to be a Member of Committee, unless he give intimation to the Preses to the effect that he would not accept of it, he shall be fined in the same manner as if he refused the office, as the Committee must be filled up before leaving the Meeting; and every Member, whether in town or country, must perform Committee duty in his turn, or pay the fine. The Clerk or Secretary and officer shall be chosen in the way the Society may think most proper, and have such salary for their trouble as the Society and they agree.

FINES FOR NON-ACCEPTANCE OF OFFICE.

XII. Any Member who may be duly elected Preses, and does not accept the office, shall pay a fine of Five Shillings sterling; and any Member chosen Treasurer, and who does not accept of it, shall also pay a fine of Five Shillings sterling; and those Members whose turn it is to be taken from the roll by rotation for Committee Members, refusing to serve, shall pay a fine of Three Shillings sterling. No Member who willingly accepted of any of these offices shall have it in his power to throw it up by paying the fine, but must continue his appointed time, unless hindered by want of health, or being unexpectedly called to the country, to reside for a continuance of time; and, in either of these cases, the office shall be taken off his hand, without demanding the fine, and another put in his place. All Members who reside in the country must pay for not serving on the Committee when it comes to their turn by rotation on the roll.

B

DUTY OF PRESES.

XIII. The Preses shall act as overseer of the Society, and see that all the Society's business is conducted conform to their regulations, and shall convene all Meetings of the Society and Committee, and preside at said Meetings of the Society and Committee; he shall also convene a full Meeting of the Society, with the advice of the Committee, when necessary. The Preses shall have all speeches addressed to him; and none shall speak but one at a time, and that when standing and uncovered, and in direct reference to the question or business before the Society, and shall not speak again on the same subject, unless he has occasion to return an answer to observations made on the subject; and, as a mark of the Society's esteem for the office-bearers, they shall respect them while in that office, and by their authority and good example do every thing in their power to promote that good order and harmony which is so very essential to the interest of the Society; and any Member usurping the prerogative of the Preses, by interrupting a Member when speaking, or otherwise behaving disorderly, shall be called to order by the Preses, whose order shall be imperative; and any Member disregarding his authority shall be fined Sixpence for the first transgression; and if again repeated, he shall be fined One Shilling; and if he still continue disorderly, he must leave the Meeting, and be fined a sum not exceeding Five Shillings; and in all questions the Preses shall have the casting vote, when votes are at a par. The Preses shall likewise order the Treasurer to pay money to the Visitors of the sick, and for funerals, &c.

FINE ON PRESES FOR NEGLECT OF DUTY.

XIV. If the Preses neglect to order the Visiting Stewards to visit the sick, when application is made to him, or neglect to order the Treasurer to pay the Sick or Funeral-money when due, or does not attend at the burying-ground, or appoint another in his absence, to receive the schedules of attending Members, he shall be fined One Shilling sterling for each neglect.

DUTY OF TREASURER.

XV. The Treasurer must find caution for his intromissions, as the Act directs, by granting a bond before beginning to act in the form therein directed; he shall receive all the money due to the Society; pay all legal charges upon it, by order of the Preses, for which he shall be accountable to the Society or Committee each quarter-day, or when required to do so; he shall likewise take charge of all papers, books, bills or bonds, or other property belonging to the Society, or whatever may be by them put under his care; he shall also, along with the Committee appointed to audit the books with the Clerk, make out the annual statement herein aftermentioned. If the Treasurer neglect to pay the Sick-money to the Visiting Stewards, when due, or does not pay the Funeral-money of a Member, or Member's wife, or widow, when ordered by the Preses, he shall be fined One Shilling for the first neglect, and Two for the second, and so on for every neglect.

DUTY OF KEY-MASTERS.

XVI. The Key-masters shall each of them have a key of the Society's Box, and must always be present when the Box is opened; and shall collect the money at Quarter or Committee Meetings, and deliver it to the Treasurer. In their absence it shall be done by some of the Committee.

DUTY OF COMMITTEE.

XVII. The ordinary Members of Committee, two of which are to be named for each month, shall visit the distressed or sick Members as soon as the Preses gives them notice of any being in distress; and they shall come and report the state of the sick or distressed to the Preses, and pay them their weekly allowance, if found entitled to it. The Visitors shall always report when they see cause, and return the book to the Preses on the day their period of duty ends, that he may send it next day by the Officer to the Visitors who next succeed. Members of Committee shall assist in all things that concern the interest or management of the Society, and be always ready to correct all mistakes and abuses that may occur, for the well-being of the Society.

DUTY OF CLERK.

XVIII. The Clerk or Secretary is to keep the Roll, Minute, and principal Cash Books of the Society and Committee; write the schedules by order of the Preses; read and write the minutes; call the roll in full when votes are taken; balance the books once a quarter, and attend all Quarterly, Committee, and other Meetings of the Society, or in any thing the Society may stand in need of his service; and it shall also be his duty to make the returns of sickness and mortality herein after provided for; and sign the books and minutes along with the Preses.

DUTY OF OFFICER.

XIX. The Officer shall be at the command of the Preses, to warn all the Members to all Meetings and Funerals within the bounds of warning, and attend all Meetings and Committees, as well as Quarterly Meetings;

he shall likewise call on the Preses once a-week, and at the change of the Visitors, convey the books to those Visitors who may next succeed ; and, if it be found necessary, attend at the burying-ground, to receive the schedules from those Members who may attend the funeral.

DUTY OF SURGEON.

XX. That a respectable medical practitioner, residing within one mile of the Cross of Edinburgh, shall be appointed Surgeon to this Society, with such salary as can be agreed on. He shall visit any Member applying for allowance, at the request of the Preses or Visiting Stewards, and according to his report, the allowance will be paid or withheld. The Surgeon's visits, upon the Society's account, shall only be for the purpose of ascertaining the Applicant's state of health, without giving either advice or medicines ; and should he be employed by any individual Member, the Society shall not be responsible for any advice or medicine that may be given him.

FINES FOR MEMBERS OF COMMITTEE NOT ATTENDING.

XXI. The Preses, Treasurer, Key-masters, and Committe shall regularly attend every Meeting at a quarter of an hour after the time appointed for the meeting ; and if any of them are absent, they shall be fined as follows, viz.—Preses, One Shilling ; Treasurer, Ninepence ; Key-masters, Sixpence ; and if their key is not sent, Sixpence more ; the other Members of Committee, Sixpence each, and no excuse shall be admitted except personal or family distress ; but at the Quarterly Meetings of the Society, if any of the above Members of Committee come in within one-half hour from the above time, they shall only pay one-half of the above fines ; but this indulgence shall not be granted at Extraordinary or Committee Meetings. Any Member who may be appointed on any extra Committee not attending within a quarter of an hour after the time appointed, shall be fined Sixpence. If a Key-master loses his key, he shall not only replace the same, but make up any loss the Society may sustain by his negligence.

FINES OF VISITORS OF THE SICK.

XXII. If the Visitors neglect to visit the sick Members, or do not pay their weekly aliment on the day it is due, or neglect to report their condition to the Preses, they shall be fined, for the first neglect, Sixpence, and for the second, One Shilling, unless a reasonable excuse is given. All fines to be paid immediately, or at the first quarter-day, and are to go to the Funds of the Society.

FINE OF CLERK AND OFFICER.

XXIII. If the Clerk is absent one quarter of an hour after the time of meeting, he shall be fined Sixpence; and if the books are not sent, Two Shillings more. If the Clerk commits any mistake by not keeping the books regular, and the Society sustain any loss by it, he shall make it up, or it shall be detained from his salary, as the Society cannot loss for his negligence. If the Officer is absent at the hour of meeting, he shall be fined Sixpence; and if absent altogether, a Sixpence more ; and if he neglect to warn any Member when ordered to do so, or neglect to change the Visitors' book, he shall be fined Sixpence for each neglect.

SOCIETY'S BOX.

XXIV. The Society shall have a Box, with three different locks and keys, into which all papers, books, money, bills, bonds, and any other securities belonging to the Society, shall be kept; the Preses to keep one key, and the other two Key-masters to have one each; which Box shall always be kept by the Treasurer, who must be a householder, and resident within one mile of the Cross of Edinburgh.

MEMBERS NECESSARY TO FORM A QUORUM.

XXV. At all Meetings, either Ordinary or Extraordinary, twenty-one Members shal form a quorum, and every deed passed at such meeting shall be as legal as if the whole Members had been present ; five Members shall likewise be a quorum of the Standing Committee.

QUARTERLY ACCOUNTS, AND FINES FOR NON-PAYMENTS.

XXVI. Each Member shall pay Two Shillings sterling as his quarter-account, ; and for each quarter-account not paid on the quarter-day, or on the Committee held after that day, Twopence shall be added to each quarter-account ; and at no time can any partial payment be taken ; and every Member must pay his quarter-accounts and other dues though sick or lame, with all fines legally exacted from them by the rules of this Society.

TIME ALLOWED FOR CLEARING THE BOOKS.

XXVII. Any Member residing within the bounds of warning, that is, within the tolls round Edinburgh, neglecting to pay up his quarters' account with expense and additions thereto, legally exacted, for full four quarters ; or if he resides at a greater distance, neglect to pay for five quarters, he shall be expelled the Society, and declared to have forfeited all claims to the Funds thereof; and, moreover, he shall forfeit all claims this Society confers upon him, and his badge taken from him, and be prosecuted for the arrears that he may be then due; and if the said Member wishes then to continue still a Member of the Society, after paying all arrears due to the Society; then, in this case, the Society shall take it into consideration, and shall restore him into all the privileges and benefits of the Society, upon paying a fine of Two Shillings and Sixpence for the trouble he has put them to, if they see cause, and if he has not been troublesome in former times. When any Member is struck off the roll, it must be recorded in the minutes of the Society at the time that it is done; but any Member who is liable to be struck off must, before that is done, be especially informed of his situation before the quarter-day, on which his name is struck off; and any Member residing in the country, and known where, shall have the same warning, if he has left his address, and if not, the Society is not to blame, he shall forfeit all claims on the Funds of the Society, and shall be dealt with accordingly for his neglect.

SECURITY FOR MEMBERS SENDING THEIR PAYMENTS.

XXVIII. Any Member sending his quarter-accounts must send his schedule along with the money, and get it discharged by the Clerk; any neglecting to do so will be liable to any loss that may arise from not attending to this order; and any Member receiving a Member's money, and not paying, but appropriating it to his own use, shall be fined Two Shillings by the Society, and shall be obliged to make up any loss that his brother may sustain by his doing so; but the Society shall not be accountable for any such mistakes or losses.

APPLICATION OF SOCIETY'S FUNDS.

XXIX. The Funds of the Society shall only be applied to the purposes of the Society, as declared in the first Article hereof, and for paying any necessary expense attending the management thereof; and any wilful misapplication of the Funds shall be punished by the expulsion from the Society of the party so offending, and forfeiture of any benefit to be derived by him, or any belonging to him, from the Society, besides being prosecuted for the money that may be misapplied.

SICK-MONEY.

XXX. No Member can have any claim on the Sick-allowance until he has been one full year and six months a Member, and clear on the books; and then, if he fall sick or lame by the visitation of Providence, and not by intemperance, or any other vice that may disable him, he shall send a line to the Preses, as follows :—

Edinburgh,   18
SIR,—*Being totally unable to follow my usual employment, by reason (here describe the disease), I do declare myself upon the benefit of the Porters' Friendly Society.*
   No.   *Street.*   *Signature.*

The Preses shall then order the Visiting Stewards to visit him, and if they are satisfied that the said Member is entitled to the Society's Sick-allowance, he shall be paid on the seventh day after application (the day of application being counted the first) Four Shillings sterling per week for thirteen weeks ; and if he is not recovered during that time, he shall be allowed Three Shillings sterling for other thirteen weeks ; and if he is still unable to follow his usual employment, he shall be allowed Two Shillings sterling for other thirteen weeks ; and if his indisposition still continues, he shall be allowed One Shilling sterling for other thirteen weeks, per week; and as the Society gives no more of these high aliments when a Member has run out the full year, and still continues in trouble, in that case, if he wishes to continue on the Society, he shall only receive Sixpence per week as superannuated money during his trouble ; and when he is on the superannuated list, he shall not be visited by the Stewards, and he can get his money weekly or quarterly as it seems good to him ; but any Member who is on the superannuated list, can draw no more of the high allowance of the Society, although he recovers, until he is one year and six months off the Fund, and in good health, and following his usual employment ; and any superannuated Member, when receiving his Sixpence per week, may do any little bodily employment to help himself; and it is understood that Members may return to their employment at any time, without waiting the expiry of a week, by giving notice thereof to the Preses before doing so, and shall receive in proportion of the allowance that he was receiving at the time, although it be in the middle of the week, by giving twenty-four hours' notice before going to work, or forfeit two weeks' aliment, at the rate he was on, for not giving the above notice.

TIME FOR BEING OFF THE SICK-ALLOWANCE.

XXXI. The Society agrees, in order that the funds may be distributed as equally as possible, that no Member shall receive any more of the high allowance than what is mentioned in the foregoing article, in the course of one year, although, from intermitting ailments, or from other causes, they may go off and come on several times in that space ; and in case of getting better any time before the above-mentioned times are complete, and applying again within the space of a year, instead of beginning again at the high allowance afresh, he shall only commence at the first, or second, or third, or last allowance, as at the time when he went off the sick list before. No Member can come on the high allowance again, unless he has been one year and six months off the Funds of the Society, and able to follow his usual employment during that time.

MEMBERS ENTITLED TO SICK-MONEY.

XXXII. No Member who runs in arrears two quarters' account, and entering on the third, shall be entitled to Sick-allowance, until the next quarter-day, and has cleared the books ; and when he pays up all his quarters and arrears, from that time only will he be entitled to his aliment, as mentioned in Art. XXX. ; and any country Member who may make application, must do it free of all expense. When any Member makes application, the Preses must see if that Member is entitled, in order that the Society's money be not misapplied. All applications must be made to the Preses in writing, and free of all expenses to the Society.

MEMBERS APPLYING WHOSE CASE IS DOUBTFUL.

XXXIII. If a Member shall make application to the Preses for his weekly supply, whose case is doubtful to the Visiting Steward, he shall desire the Surgeon to go and see him, and, according to his report, the allowance will be paid or withheld. If his distemper is found to be feigned, or the result of excessive drinking, fighting, quarrelling, or vice of any kind, or arising from irregular or disorderly conduct ; or if he be found working at his daily employment, or at any employment whatever, while receiving the Society's aliment, the said Member shall, upon any of these offences being proved, be expelled the Society, and lose all the privileges thereof ; and if any Member be aiding or assisting in drawing money for such a person, knowing of such imposition, he or they so offending, shall be fined Twenty Shillings sterling, or expelled the Society.

MEMBERS RECEIVING SICK-ALLOWANCE.

XXXIV. No Member is allowed to do any bodily labour, or to follow after his ordinary employment, when receiving Sick-money ; and every Member on the Society's allowance, must give intimation to the Preses of his intention of going to work one day before he tries it; if he goes to work before he gives intimation, although it be the first day he does so, he shall be fined two weeks' Sick-money, at the rate he was on at the time ; and, likewise, any Member upon the Sick-allowance, who shall behave disorderly, or be intoxicated with liquor, or found out of his lodgings after nine o'clock at night, without giving a satisfactory reason to the Society or the Committee, shall be suspended from the allowance of the Society, until his conduct be considered at the first quarter-day meeting thereafter; and if the charges are proved against him, he shall receive no Sick-money during his indisposition, or for such other time as the Society see cause.

MEMBERS GIVING UP SICK ALLOWANCE.

XXXV. Any Member upon the Sick-allowance thinking himself recovered, and giving up the Society's allowance, must, before beginning to work, give in a line to the Preses in writing, stating the sum he has received during his trouble; and any Member who has received aliment during the quarter is to give in a line on the quarter-day, to the following effect :—

Edinburgh,   18

Sir,—*I acknowledge to have received   weeks' and   days' aliment this quarter, and have been regularly paid and visited.*

Signature.

Any person neglecting to do so shall forfeit One Shilling.

SICK-MONEY TO COUNTRY MEMBERS.

XXXVI. As the Visitors can only visit within the bounds of warning, every Member residing without said bounds requesting Sick-money, if entitled to it, must certify by the minister and two elders of the parish, or by the minister and two elders of the religious community to which he may belong to, by a certificate, (a form of which is hereafter added,) and likewise a surgeon, if he has any attending him, mentioning the nature of his disease, and when he was unable to follow his employment, which shall be deemed sufficient evidence to entitle him to the Society's allowance, and which shall be paid to any person he may appoint, who shall give a receipt for it; and if residing above twenty miles, and within fifty miles of Edinburgh, the application must be made within two weeks from the date he was rendered unable to work ; and if residing above that distance, said certificate must be sent within three weeks from the date he was first laid aside from his employment ; and, in either of those cases, if more time elapse, the Society is not bound to pay the over time ; and the said certificate must be repeated each time the Member has occasion for the aliment, which must not be above a month after the first one sent, and free of all expense to the Society. When a Member, who is without the bounds of warning, has been on the sick list and recovered, his last attestation must be sent before he goes to work, as likewise his statement in full, acknowledging the sums he has received during his illness ; and if he neglects to do so till after he is at work, he will not be entitled

C

to any aliment on such a certificate, and be liable to the fine for not giving a return of the number of weeks' aliment he has received. No Member can receive or demand any allowance of Sick-money, if he has neglected to do so in time of trouble, after he has recovered, for the past time in which he was badly.

INTIMATION OF THE DEATH OF A MEMBER.

XXXVII. When any free Member, his wife or widow, dies, within the bounds of warning, intimation thereof must be made in writing, and the time of interment specified, and sent to the Preses in proper time, so as he may have forty-eight hours to make out schedules to warn the Society's Members to attend the funeral; and in case such relations do not wish the Members of the Society to attend the funeral, or do not give such intimation as above stated, they shall forfeit Fifteen Shillings sterling of the Funeral-money, as the Society wish to see all their deceased Members decently interred.

SUM ALLOWED FOR FUNERALS.

XXXVIII. Upon the death of a free Member, the Preses shall order the Treasurer to pay the sum of Four Pounds sterling to his widow, or next of kin, as Funeral-money, and for a wife or widow, Three Pounds sterling, as Funeral-money, shall be paid to the husband, or next of kin ; and at the receiving of any of these sums, a receipt in the books must be given by the husband, widow, or next of kin who receive it. The Treasurer, or any of the Visitors, shall pay the above sums before or after the interment. If a Member be indebted to the Society at the time of his own or his wife's death, the debt shall be deducted from the Funeral-money ; and, to assist in defraying the expense of every funeral, each Member is to pay Sixpence for each Member, or Member's wife, or widow's Funeral, the first quarter-day after such funeral shall have taken place, in addition to the other contribution to be made by Members as before-mentioned.

MEMBERS DYING IN THE COUNTRY.

XXXIX. If a Member lawfully depart from Edinburgh to any other part of the nation, and he or his wife die there, a certificate must be sent, signed by the Minister of the place, and the Recorder of the bills of mortality, where the deceased was buried, and sent to the Preses, who will then order the Funeral-money to be paid to the person that may be appointed to receive it, upon granting a discharge for the same in the funeral receipt-book of the Society, and free of all expenses to the Society.

MEMBERS OR WIDOWS DYING HAVING NO RELATIONS.

XL. Should a Member or widow die in Edinburgh, and have no relations or friends to take charge of the funeral, or should they decline to interfere, the Preses, in either of these cases, shall take the management, and see that the funeral be properly conducted, conform to the spirit and intentions of these articles.

MEMBERS ATTENDING FUNERALS.

XLI. When a Member, his wife, or widow, dies within the bounds of warning, intimation being given to the Preses, he shall order the Clerk to warn the portion of the Members allowed of the Society from the roll, by rotation to attend ; and every Member in health residing within the bounds of warning, shall attend when it is his turn, either at the funeral of a Member, his wife, or widow, belonging to the Society, if he is warned to attend the evening before the funeral. Any Member, whose turn it is, and does not attend in his most suitable apparel, shall be fined Sixpence ; and every Member attending a funeral must give his schedule to the Preses, or the person whom he may appoint in his absence, at the burying-ground, after the interment ; also, it is expressly declared, that at any of the before-mentioned funerals, when the Members are warned, and attend, that every Member so attending shall have it in his power to deliver up his schedule to the person appointed to receive them, if the funeral does not move off within twenty minutes after the time stated in the schedule ; and if any Member comes to a funeral intoxicated with liquor, or improperly dressed, he shall leave the funeral immediately, by order of the Members present, and be fined in One Shilling, and if obstinate, and do not leave, he shall be fined Two Shillings for his disgraceful conduct.

MEMBERS RE-MARRYING.

XLII. It is expressly understood the Society allows no Funeral-money but to one wife, unless every Member, when he marries a second wife (after having once been allowed Funeral-money), shall pay into the Funds of the Society the sum of One Pound sterling, and must be married three years ; and in case of a third, Two Pounds sterling, and be married three years ; and so on in all such re-marrying, and all said sums must be paid within three months after such marriage, as Funeral-money, when it shall take place, and if any Member's wife dies within said three years from their marriage, he shall only receive the sum that was paid in name of Funeral-money ; and any Member not complying with these rules, will not be entitled to have his wife or widow buried by the Society. Any Member wishing to comply with this rule, must give in his wife's maiden name.

RULES FOR WIDOWS.

XLIII. That every widow whom the Society is bound to bury, and who wishes to continue upon the Society for the benefit of her Funeral-money, must, upon every Whitsunday quarter and November quarter, pay into the Funds of the Society, a Sixpence each term, as before-mentioned, and produce a certificate each time, if required, signed by the Minister and two Elders of the religious community she belongs to, that she is still the widow of the Society's deceased Member; and if living within the bounds of warning, she shall be warned by the Officer before every term-day; and if residing without the bounds of warning, she may, if desired, be warned by post; and any widow changing her place of residence, must give notice to the Preses thereof, and if any neglect to do so, the Society shall not be accountable for any loss she may sustain. If a widow neglect, or refuse, to certify her widowhood after the second intimation so to do, or neglect to pay for two years, it shall be considered she has relinquished her claim for Funeral-money, and shall be scored off the roll of widows, and can have no more claim on the Society. If any widow neglects to pay her half-yearly Sixpence, one penny shall be added to it. Any widow forming an illicit connexion with any man, forfeits her right to Funeral-money. Any widow dying without the bounds of warning, her death must be certified by the Minister of the parish, and two Elders of the religious community she belongs to, certifying that she died the widow of the Society's deceased Member; and any widow who marries a Member of the Society, although he may die before becoming a free Member, her Funeral-money, as a widow, shall still be secured to her, if her former husband was a free Member at the time of his death. Any widow marrying a person, not a Member of the Society, forfeits her claim to any Funeral-money. Any Member who marries a widow belonging to this Society, who had a claim to the Society's Funeral-money, in this case shall not be called upon to pay the sums mentioned in Art. XLII., although she may happen to be his second or third wife.

MEMBERS CHANGING THEIR PLACE OF RESIDENCE.

XLIV. Any Member changing his place of residence, must give notice thereof in writing to the Preses, that he may be warned to any meeting or funeral; but if he neglect to do so, he shall be liable to the same fine as if duly warned.

STANDING FUNDS OF THE SOCIETY.

XLV. If the Funds of the Society shall happen to be reduced to One Hundred Pounds sterling, every Member binds and obliges himself to pay Sixpence in addition to the usual quarter-accounts, until the Funds amount to One Hundred and Twenty Pounds sterling, when the quarter-accounts shall fall to their original amount; but at no time can the Members entitled be deprived of the benefit of the Society's Sick-money; but in case the Funds fall below the standing Funds of the Society, in this case the Society shall be empowered to call a meeting to consider the state of the Funds, and to give out the aliment according to the state of their Funds, by giving the second or third rate, as mentioned in Article XXX., until the Funds amount to the above-mentioned sum ; the Society shall have it in their power to rise or lower the Sick or Funeral-money as the Funds will admit, provided all such alterations of these Rules, and of the rates hereby fixed, shall de duly intimated to, and agreed upon by three-fourths of the Society, and sanctioned in terms of law.

SECURING THE SOCIETY'S PROPERTY.

XLVI. In order to prevent, as much as possible, the Funds of the Society from being embezzled, or misapplied, no money shall be lent out, or invested, without the direction of the Society at one of the General Meetings thereof, and all bills, bonds, and other securities, shall be taken in name of the Preses and Treasurer, for the time being, as trustees for behoof of the Society ; and no money shall be lent to any Member, or private individual, but shall be lodged in one of the public chartered Banks, or invested in heritable property, or in one or other of the securities specified in the Act of the 10th Geo. IV. cap. 56 ; and if any Member shall embezzle any of the Society's money, he shall not only refund the same, but pay a fine of Five Shillings sterling ; and if it is proved to the satisfaction of the Society, that any Member is guilty of a designed fraud, by which the Society might suffer loss, he shall make good the loss, and be expelled the Society, as afore-mentioned. , The whole effects and property of the Society are hereby declared to be vested in the Preses and Treasurer, for the time being, as trustees for the Society, hereby appointed for that purpose ; and, when necessary, these parties, as trustees, shall sue, and be sued, in name and for behoof of the Society, according to section twenty-one of the Act of the 10th Geo. IV. cap. 56.

CALUMNIATING OF OFFICE-BEARERS OR MEMBERS.

XLVII. If any Member shall upbraid another, who has received benefit from the Society when entitled to it, without cause, or shall raise an unjust calumny upon any of the Office-bearers, in the discharge of their duty, he shall, for the first offence, be publicly rebuked by the Preses before the Society, and pay a fine of Two Shillings and Sixpence ; and for the second offence, Five Shillings; and if offending a third time, he shall be expelled the Society, as an unworthy Member, and forfeit all the money he has paid, and can have no more claim on the Society, according to the spirit of the Society's Rules or Laws.

MEMBERS EMIGRATING, OR CALLED ABROAD ON BUSINESS.

XLVIII. As emigration has become so common in this country, any Member leaving Great Britain, with a view to reside abroad, and taking his family along with him (if he has one,) in that case he shall no longer be considered a Member of this Society, nor shall his quarter-accounts be received from his friends or others whom he may appoint to pay them ; but if he return in perfect health within three years, and pay his arrears, due during his absence, he shall again be received into the Society ; but should a Member be called abroad in the course of business, and his family or others whom he may appoint, pay his quarter-accounts, &c. in this case his Funeral-money shall be secured to him ; but no Sick-money shall be paid while he is residing out of Great Britain and Ireland; and if his family or others neglect to pay his quarters' account, he shall be dealt with according to the regulation stated in Article XXVIII.

EXCLUSION OF MEMBERS CONVICTED OF THEFT.

XLIX. When a Member shall be judicially convicted of theft, or any other crime inferring infamy and moral depravity, he shall therefore be deprived of all further connection with the Society, and shall forfeit all he has contributed to the Funds, and be expelled the Society as an unworthy Member.

DISPUTES AND ARBITRATION.

L. In order to prevent disputes and law-suits betwixt this Society and its Members, they shall endeavour, to the utmost of their power, to act with candour and impartiality in all causes that may come before them ; they therefore agree, that if any Member shall think himself wronged by any deed of the Committee or Society, he may appeal to a full meeting of the Society ; and if he still thinks he is wronged, he shall be allowed to appeal to the Society a second time, at their next full meeting; but should he still be dissatisfied with the decision of the Society, he shall have no resort to any Court of Law; but it is hereby declared, that should any dispute still continue to exist between the Society, or any person acting under them, and any individual Member thereof, or any person claiming on account of any Member thereof, such dispute shall be referred to arbitrators, and the determination of said arbitrators shall be final to all intents and purposes, as directed by the Act of Parliament (19th June 1829,) 10th Geo. IV. cap. 56, sect. 27, without appeal, or being subject to the control of any Court of Law or Equity, their decree to be given forth or pronounced, if possible, within three months from the date of submission ; the award of the arbiters to be enforced in the manner directed by the foresaid Act of Parliament.

MANNER OF CHOOSING ARBITRATORS.

LI. For this purpose there shall be chosen, at the first meeting of the Society, after the confirmation of these rules, a body of arbitrators, consisting of nine persons, none of whom being beneficially interested in the affairs of the Society, whose names shall be entered in the Society's books ; and in every case of dispute, three arbitrators will be chosen by ballot to decide the same. The mode of ballot will be as follows:— The names of the nine arbitrators shall be put into a box, written on separate or similar pieces of paper, and three of them shall be taken out of the box by the Preses of the Meeting at which the dispute shall come on for being settled, which three persons shall proceed to decide the dispute in question.

AUDITING THE BOOKS.

LII. Upon the head quarter-day in November annually, there shall be chosen a Select Committee of three Members, to audit the books for the preceding year, who, with the Clerk, shall make out and audit a general statement of the income and expenditure of the Society for the bygone year, containing all the particulars mentioned in the 33d clause of the foresaid Act of Geo. IV. cap. 56, to which reference is hereto especially made, and which general statement shall be attested by two or more of the said auditors, and counter-signed by the Clerk, and distributed on the February quarter first following, and every Member shall be entitled to receive a copy of such annual statement on payment of Sixpence ; and the Society shall, every five years, make out a return of the sickness and mortality experienced by the Society, within the before-mentioned period of five years, according to the form prescribed in Schedule (A,) appended to the Act of Parliament, 10th Geo. IV. cap. 56, a copy of which is annexed to these Rules and Regulations.

ALTERATIONS AND AMENDMENTS.

LIII. It is provided that, at any General Meeting, any additions, alterations, or amendments proposed shall be laid before the Society in writing, when the same shall be taken under consideration, and if approved of, shall lie on the table until the next Meeting, and if then approved of by three-fourths of the Society, it shall be adopted as a part of the rules of this Society, when duly intimated, submitted, agreed to, and sanctioned in terms of the Act of Parliament. (See in particular sections 7 and 9 of the said Act.)

TO PREVENT THE DISSOLUTION OF THE SOCIETY.

LIV. That it shall not be lawful, by any rule, order, or regulation, at any General Meeting of the Society, or otherwise, to dissolve the same, so long as the purposes for which it was established, or any of them, remain to be carried into effect, without the consent of five-sixths in number of the then existing Members, every Member being entitled to one vote, and an additional vote for every five years that he may have been a Member, provided, however, that no Member shall have more than five votes in whole, and also the consent of all persons receiving or entitled to receive any of the Society's allowance.

MEMBERS TO PURCHASE SOCIETY'S RULES AND REGULATIONS.

LV. Every Member shall purchase a copy of these Articles, that none may pretend ignorance of the Laws and Regulations of this Society. The books of the Society shall be at all seasonable times open to the Members, and particularly at all General Meetings of the Society. The Society shall at all times have in their possession a copy of the Act, in order that it may be referred to upon all occasions for the government and guidance of their affairs, and they shall in all things conform to its provisions ; a copy of the Act, along with these Rules, being bound up in a book, to be kept in the box, or with the Preses for the time being ; and Members and entrants shall subscribe the same, in token of their adherence thereto.

WIDOWS CLAIMING FUNERAL-MONEY WHILE IN LIFE.

LVI. And be it enacted, that any widow who wishes to have her Funeral-money from this Society, while in life, may make application to the Society at any of their General or Committee Meetings of the Society, and then the Society or Committee shall consider the state of the applicant's claim, and if they see cause, they may grant One Pound Ten Shillings sterling, to be paid to the applicant as Funeral-money, on a proper receipt being given in their book, that the applicant has no more claim on the Society, or any other person claiming for the same, in all time coming ; but the Society have it in their power to give or refuse it.

MEMBERS HAVE IT IN THEIR POWER TO LEAVE THE SOCIETY.

LVII. Any who may wish to give up their contributions to this Society, must do so by giving a line in writing to the Preses, stating that they have no more claim on the Society's Funds, and paying all arrears that they may be then due the Society, and giving up their badge ; any neglecting to do so shall be prosecuted for whatever they may be due the Society, while they keep the Society's property, or any privilege the Society has conferred on them.

FORM OF CERTIFICATE FOR COUNTRY MEMBERS.

We, the undersigned, do hereby certify, to our personal knowledge, that   , a Member of The Town Porters' Friendly Society of Edinburgh, has lived in the (town or village) of   , parish of   , county of   , during which time he has behaved himself soberly, honestly, and orderly ; and, by reason of (here name the disease) he is unable, since   , to follow after his usual employment, or any other employment : That his disorder does not proceed from any vicious or disorderly conduct, nor brought on himself by intemperance, is attested by us, on soul and conscience,

Minister of the parish of   or Religious
Community residing in   parish or street.
Surgeon.

D

PENALTIES.

(All Fines to go to the Funds of the Society.)

That the following shall be the penalties for a breach of the foregoing laws, and the cases after-mentioned :—

1. *Absence from Meetings.*

Preses absent one quarter of an hour after the time of meeting £0	1	0		
Treasurer do. do.	0	0	9
Key-masters do. do.	0	0	6
Do. absent, and not sending their key, additional	0	0	6
Committee Members absent as above . . .	0	0	6
Clerk do. do. . . .	0	0	6
Do. absent, if the books are not sent . . .	0	2	0
Officer absent at the hour of meeting · . .	0	0	6
Do. if absent altogether, additional . . .	0	0	6
Do. not giving the book to the Visitors . .	0	0	6
Members absent at the head quarter or election . .	0	1	0
Do. at Extraordinary Meetings . .	0	0	6
Do. when appointed on extra Committees .	0	0	6
Members leaving a meeting without leave asked and granted	0	0	3

2. *Neglect of Duty.*

Preses neglecting to order Treasurer to pay Sick or Funeral-money, &c. . . . . · .	0	1	0
Do. to give orders for warning the Society to a Funeral	0	2	6
Treasurer neglecting, when ordered, to pay Sick or Funeral-money	0	1	0
Visiting Stewards neglecting to visit sick and pay them, first offence	0	0	6
Do. do. second offence	0	1	0
Members who have been, or who are on the sick list, not intimating the number of weeks they have received, on or before the quarter-day	0	1	0

3. *Not accepting of Office.*

Members refusing to serve as Preses	.	.	.	0	5	0
Do.	do.	Treasurer	.	0	5	0
Do.	do.	Key-masters	.	0	3	0
Do. not serving on Committee by rotation		.		0	3	0

4. *General Fines.*

Members not attending funerals . . . 0 0 6

Do. not paying each quarter-account . . 0 0 2

Do. intoxicated with liquor, and disturbing meeting, first
offence 0 0 6

Do. do. second offence 0 1 0

Do. fraudulently aiding or assisting any Member to draw
Sick-money when not entitled to it . . . 1 0 0

Do. embezzling any part of the funds . . 0 5 0

Do. calumniating Office-bearers, or raising unjust reports,
first offence 0 2 6

Do. do. second offence 0 5 0

5. *Forfeiture of Sick-Money.*

Members going to work before giving intimation one day before doing so, forfeit two weeks' Sick-money.

Members on the Sick List intoxicated with liquor, or found out of their lodgings after nine o'clock at night, without due cause, forfeit Sick-money for that trouble, or such other time as the Society see cause.

6. *Expulsion and Forfeiture of Contributions.*

Imposing on the Society by underrating his age three or more years, or fraudulent concealment of disease at entry.

Embezzlement of the Funds, and fraudulent misapplication thereof, and to be prosecuted for restitution of the same.

Imposing on the Society by feigning sickness, or otherwise fraudulently obtaining money from the Society.

Non-payment of Members within the bounds of warning four quarters.

Do. do. without the bounds of warning five quarters.

GENERAL RULES.

Every Member, wife, or widow receiving Funeral-money from this Society, shall pay Two Shillings sterling to the Officer for delivering the funeral schedules to warn the Members to attend the funeral of a Member, wife, or widow.

Any Member of this Society, through old age, who is not able to work at his usual employment, if in good bodily health, cannot come on the full aliment of this Society, but must apply at one of their General Meetings, and state his case, and then they will take his case into their consideration, and allow him what they may judge proper, or the state of the Funds will admit of.

Edinburgh, 28*th February* 1833.

WE, the undersigned Committee, appointed by the Society to revise the former articles, having met and duly considered the same, do unanimously agree to submit the foregoing for the Society's approbation and approval.

> DUNCAN M'MARTIN, *Preses.*
> DONALD ROBERTSON, *Treasurer.*
> JOHN M'MILLAN.
> THOMAS BAILLIE.
> JAMES M'CABE.
> PATRICK CASEY.
> DANIEL DEMPESY.
> JAMES HEWITT, *Clerk.*

Edinburgh, 8*th March* 1833.

The forementioned Rules and Regulations having been twice read over at Special Meetings called for that purpose, were approven of, and a clean copy directed to be made out for the Society, to be certified and sanctioned in terms of the Act of the 10th Geo. IV. cap. 56.

> DUNCAN M'MARTIN, *Preses.*
> DONALD ROBERTSON, *Treasurer.*
> JOHN M'MILLAN.
> THOMAS BAILLIE.
> JAMES HEWITT, *Clerk.*

EDINBURGH, 32, INDIA STREET,
3d April 1833.

I hereby certify that I have perused the foregoing Rules of " The Town Porters' Friendly Society," (Edinburgh,) each page of which is subscribed with my initials in reference hereto, and that the same are in conformity to law, and to the provisions of the Act of the 10th Geo. IV. chap. 56, intituled, " An Act to Consolidate and Amend the Laws relating to Friendly Societies."

AND. MURRAY *jun.*
Advocate-Depute appointed to certify
the Rules of Friendly Societies.

Edinburgh, 30*th April* 1833.

BEING A GENERAL QUARTER SESSIONS.

The meeting having considered the Articles and Regulations for governing " The Town Porters' Friendly Society," with the certificate of the Advocate-Depute thereto attached, allowed and confirmed the same accordingly.

(Signed)   JAS. AITKEN, *Dep. Clerk.*

SCHEDULE (A).

LIST of the MEMBERS of THE TOWN PORTERS' FRIENDLY SOCIETY, held at Edinburgh, established on the 12th day of March 1688; with a Return of the Sickness and Mortality experienced for the Period of Five Years, commencing January 1, 18 and ending December 31, 18

NAMES.	Trade, or Profession.	Date of Birth.	Date of Admission into the Society.	Date of becoming a Free Member.	For what time entitled to Relief on account of Sickness.					For what Time entitled to Relief on account of Superannuation.					Date of Death.	Place of Residence at time of Death.	REMARKS.
					In 18 Days. / Weeks.	In 18 Days. / Weeks.	In 18 Days. / Weeks.	In 18 Days. / Weeks.	In 18 Days. / Weeks.	In 18 Days. / Weeks.	In 18 Days. / Weeks.	In 18 Days. / Weeks.	In 18 Days. / Weeks.	In 18 Days. / Weeks.			
[N.B.—This Column may be filled up with the Members' Initials.]																	

RULES

FOR

A BENEFIT SOCIETY,

CALLED THE

UNITED PHILANTHROPISTS.

INSTITUTED AUGUST 6th, 1811.

AMENDED PURSUANT TO 10 GEO. IV. c. 56.

" ———— ————Mankind's concern is charity;
All must be false that thwart this one great end,
And all of God that bless mankind or mend."

POPE.

LONDON:

PRINTED BY W. DIMMEREY, 15, NEW ROAD, WHITECHAPEL.

1833.

PREAMBLE.

MANKIND being subject to calamities from various accidents, bodily infirmities, sickness, and age, it was resolved to establish this society, to consist of one hundred and fifty members; the intention of which is to support, when it shall please God to afflict any member, either with sickness, accidents, or any infirmity : and for the better securing unto us the blessings we may reasonably expect, under this laudable undertaking, let us implore Almighty God to assist us, and to strengthen our design with the comfort of brotherly love; to unite us all in the bonds of pure friendship, being the only means to accomplish the good purposes hereby intended ; and to enable us to give relief to those who are in affliction, every member shall pay certain sums of money, as the rules do specify and regulate, which contributions, as they accumulate, shall be funded in the bank of England ; and as this society desires the good of every individual member, and the general good of the whole, it is resolved that no person shall be admitted unless he is proposed by one and seconded by another of the members : he shall be a man of credit and reputation, whose character and conduct are unimpeachable ; the strictest attention, therefore, will be paid by the committee to detect any imposter, by the admission of improper persons.

RULES.

I. THIS society shall consist of one hundred and fifty members, to meet on the first Tuesday in every month, from eight till ten o'clock, but quarterly nights from seven till ten ; quarterly nights are the first Tuesdays in January, April, July, and October ; and every member, sick or well, unless exempted by any subsequent rule, shall subscribe two shillings and fivepence per month to the stock. The committee shall not be allowed to smoke till after business is over.

II. That in order to establish the respectability of this society, it is resolved that no person shall be admitted, unless he is recommended by one, and seconded by another of the members ; he shall be a man of credit and reputation, his earnings not less than twenty-four shillings per week, and not afflicted with diseases of any kind whatever; he shall not be under the age of twenty-one years, nor more than thirty years, neither shall he be a member of any other society of this nature ; such person being sufficiently qualified, to the satisfaction of the committee, shall, on the next meeting night, should he then be approved of, make the following declaration to the president:—

" I do hereby declare, upon my honour and belief, that I am in a sound state of body, free from, and not subject to any dangerous chronic disorder ; above the age of twenty-one, and not exceeding the age of thirty years ; and that I will not belong to, or receive benefit from any society of this particular nature, after I have become a free member of this."

The person shall likewise sign his name to the rules of this society, to signify that he gives his full and free consent to abide by and comform to the respective rules herein contained, so long as he shall continue a member ; and provided it should appear to this society, after the admission of any member, that he had falsely declared and imposed on the society, such member shall forfeit all monies to be continued eighteen weeks; and if the member continues in affliction for a longer period, he shall be allowed ten shillings, and to be continued at that sum for eight months; but should he declare off the fund at any period on or before the expiration of eighteen weeks, as aforesaid; and should he again become afflicted with a recurrence of the same or any other disease, he shall receive the remainder of his full pay, to complete eighteen weeks in one year, and then receive half the sum for eight months; and should he continue still in affliction, he shall be deemed a pensioner, and shall be allowed, if he has been a member seven years and under, four shillings; seven years and under fourteen years, five shillings; fourteen years and upwards, six shillings per week; but should it appear to the society that a member receiving the pension is sufficiently recovered to follow his employment, the committee shall be empowered to place him on the books, and he shall pay all fines and contributions as other members; should he continue in health for twelve months from the time of his being called on by the committee, he shall be entitled to the benefit allowed to free members; but should he be afflicted within that period, he shall be allowed his pension money only; should the afflicted member continue four weeks on the society's box, he shall send a certificate of his illness, addressed to the secretary, at the society's club house, signed by the medical person attending on him, stating the nature of his complaint; the said certificate must be renewed every four weeks, till he declares off the fund; and should he neglect to send the said certificate, he shall be fined five shillings, and receive no pay until his certificate is renewed.

X. Should any member on the fund be found working at his business or any pecuniary employment, gambling, attending convivial meetings,

paid by him into this society's fund, and he shall be for ever excluded.

III. Every person shall pay his entrance money according to his age, viz. from twenty-one to twenty-four, one pound; from twenty-four to twenty-seven, one pound ten shillings; from twenty-seven to thirty, two pounds; which sums may be paid by different instalments, as shall seem most convenient to the member; but such member must clear the books when he has been in the society twelve months; and in case any member does not make up such instalments as shall be due at the expiration of twelve months, or the meeting night after the member or members to be summoned by the secretary to attend the next meeting night, and should he fail to clear the books on that night, he shall be excluded.

IV. That whoever does not clear the books on the quarterly nights shall be fined one shilling, and the secretary shall send him notice that if he does not clear the books of all demands (due on such quarterly night) the following meeting night, he will be excluded; and if he does not clear the books agreeable to such notice, he will be excluded accordingly, and forfeit all monies paid by him into this society's fund, and the secretary shall be paid threepence for every such notice, which must be sent at least fourteen days previous to the meeting night, or he will be fined one shilling; each member to pay the postage of his letters to and from the society.

V. That the business of this society shall be conducted by a committee of six members, three of which shall go out of office every three months, (quarterly nights) and three fresh ones chosen, the call to proceed from the last committee-man, at nine o'clock precisely; those who are absent, or refuse to serve, shall pay a fine of eighteen pence, except on the fund. The committee shall meet regularly on every monthly and quarterly nights, to receive contributions and admit members, to audit the accounts, insert fines, and see that the rules are fairly acted up to, and that three members of the committee shall be sufficient to proceed to business; they shall be empowered to superintend all the concerns of the society, and to fine members for non-attendance at general meetings, not exceeding one shilling: every committee-man who is absent on any meeting night half an hour beyond the usual time of meeting, (sickness excepted) shall be fined sixpence for each neglect, and if absent the whole of the evening he shall pay the fine of one shilling; and if any committee-man shall, after accepting the office, resign, and not find a substitute, he shall be fined five shillings, and on refusal to pay such fine, he shall be excluded.

VI. That for the better regulation of this society, the president shall be ballotted for every six months, whose duty it shall be to direct the proceedings of the society, according to the tenor of the rules, to keep good order and decorum, to form such regulations in the conduct of the business of the society as he may think necessary and proper, and to see that all other officers do their duty; any member refusing to serve this office, when ballotted, shall be fined two shillings and sixpence; any member disobeying the president shall be fined one shilling, and should he still continue disorderly after being fined, the president shall order him to quit the room, and if not immediately complied with, he shall be fined eighteen pence: the president neglecting to put this rule in force, shall be fined one shilling for each neglect; and should he be absent at the opening of the society, he shall be fined one shilling; and if absent the whole of the evening, and does not send a substitue, he shall be fined two shillings, and not liable to serve the same office for twelve months.

VII. That in order to preserve as much as possible the harmony and tranquillity of the society, and to prevent litigation, it is agreed by every person who now is, and hereafter shall become a member of the society, in case any dispute arise between the society, or any person or persons acting under them, and any member or members of this society, or persons claiming on account of a member, that all disputes shall be settled before two or more justices of the peace, agreeable to an act in that case made and provided—10 Geo. 4, c. 56, s. 27-28.

VIII. Than the committee shall be allowed one shilling each per day for visiting the sick; and in order to cover such expense, each member shall subscribe twopence per month extra; but if the committee-man neglects to visit any one of the sick members within the bounds, which is three miles from the house where the society is held, he shall not be allowed any thing, and shall be fined two shillings; (sickness excepted) and if any member shall withhold, embezzle, or appropriate to his own use any of the sick member's or society's money, he shall be fined one pound one shilling, and on the next meeting night shall make good the whole of the money so embezzled, together with the fine, or be proceeded against according to law, and be excluded from the society. The committee shall be empowered to prosecute agreeable to the statute. The committee-man upon drawing the sick member's money, shall be allowed sixpence, and in the event of the sick members not receiving their money before eight o'clock on the Saturday evening, the committee-man shall be fined five shillings for each neglect.

IX. That all persons who enter this society shall be free in twelve months, and when free, shall be allowed in affliction twenty shillings per week, the payment to commence the day after he declares on the society, or in a state of intoxication, his money shall be suspended, he shall be made acquainted with the charge about to be brought against him, and summoned to attend on the next meeting night, when, if he should make it appear to the satisfaction of the majority of the members then present, that he is innocent, his arrears shall be paid to him, and he shall receive his money as before ; but if proved guilty of the charge, he shall be excluded, and forfeit all monies paid by him into the society's fund ; should the member not attend, according to summons, (sickness excepted) he will be considered guilty, and excluded accordingly.

XI. If any member shall become past his labor, or be reduced to a workhouse, on account of sickness, old age, or infirmity, he shall receive six shillings per week.

XII. If any sick member is desirous of going into an hospital, his weekly money shall be paid him the same as if at home, and to be visited by the pay-steward only ; likewise, if any member is taken ill while in the country, and desires the benefit of this society, he shall, upon sending a certificate signed by the apothecary cr surgeon attending the said member, (stating the nature of his complaint) and the minister of the parish where he shall reside, or for the want of an apothecary or surgeon, attested by the minister and churchwardens, receive all benefits as though in town. The certificate must be renewed every four weeks, and sent addressed to the secretary at the society's club house, or he will be fined five shillings, and his money will be stopped.

XIII. Form of declaring on the society--To the United Philanthropists—I,   residing at   do declare on the funds of this society, this   day of   18   being afflicted with   which renders me unable to follow my employ.

Form of declaring off the society—To the United Philanthropists—I,   residing at being, by the blessing of God, recovered from my late illness, do declare off the funds of this society, this   day of   18

XIV. That at the death of a free member, or a free member's wife, notice shall be sent to the secretary, who shall immediately inform the president, and they shall go to see the deceased, and shall take care that provision is made for a decent funeral, free from all parochial relief, and they shall likewise attend the funeral, or forfeit two shillings and sixpence ; and for their trouble, they shall be allowed three shillings each from the stock, and on the next meeting night the committee shall pay to the widow, (if any) on her producing the certificate of her marriage, or nominee, who must be a relation. If he has been a member one year, the sum of ten pounds ; if two years, fifteen pounds; and if three years, twenty pounds ; but if a free member's wife, one half the above sums. No member to receive at the death of a second wife, until the expiration of five years from the demise of the first.

XV. That when any member, through affliction, shall declare on the society's fund, he shall send his declaration, addressed to the secretary, at the society's club house, expressing the nature of his illness, the date of the month and year, his place of abode, and the secretary on receiving the notice shall send it the next day to that committee-man whose turn it is to visit, who shall the next day visit the afflicted member before eight o'clock in the evening, and leave with him a sick list for the visitors to sign their names on the days they visit, and after visiting all the sick members, he shall take the roll the same day to that committee-man whose name stands next on the roll to visit, or be fined one shilling, and one shilling for every day the sick member is not visited through such neglect.

The sick member shall be visited three times in each week, and on what days the visitors think proper, Sundays excepted. The sick member must return the sick list every monthly night, before nine o'clock, or be fined two shillings, and fresh ones to be issued out by the secretary.

XVI. That a secretary shall be chosen from the society, to continue in office for one year ; he shall be allowed twelve shillings per quarter for his trouble ; he shall regularly attend his duty, and if absent half an hour beyond his time, shall be fined sixpence ; if an hour, one shilling ; and if he does not come the whole evening or send a substitute, he shall be fined five shillings ; he shall carefully register every member's admission, residence, and removal, and likewise the death of members and their wives. He shall keep a faithful account of what monies are at different times received, and likewise what are disbursed, when and on what account, or be fined five shillings for each neglect ; he shall record the minutes of the society, and assist the committee with the best advice and counsel in his power, in whatever shall appear to him to have a tendency to the general good ; and for the information of the friends of members on the scratch, he shall post their names in a conspicuous part of the room ; and in order to secure a fair election, on all occasions, each ballot must bear his private mark.

XVII. That upon the removal of any member, he shall register his address in a book kept for such purpose at the society's club house, on or before the meeting night following such removal, or be fined one shilling.

XVIII. That no person who is employed in any pernicious trade shall be admitted a member of this society ; nor shall any lapidary, colour grinder, looking glass silverer, water gilder, painter, plumber, worker in white lead, fireman, tailor, plasterer, bricklayer, bricklayer's laborer, bailiff or bailiff's follower, thief taker, or any dangerous artificer, be admitted on any account whatever; and if any person of the above description, through artifice, has gained his admittance into this society, he shall be excluded, and forfeit all monies paid by him into the society's fund.

XIX. That for the better protection of this society, all persons having become members since the 6th day of August, 1822, who may be detected in following any of the before mentioned objectionable trades or callings, upon sufficient proof being shown to the society, he shall be excluded, and forfeit all monies paid by him into the society's fund.

XX. That every free member shall have leave to visit the sick at seasonable hours ; and any member knowing of any imposition in a drawing member, and conniving at the same, shall be fined ten shillings.

XXI. If any member's affliction is caused by the venereal disease or fighting, and it is proved that he began or was the provoker, such member shall not receive any benefit, except it should end with death, in which case, the usual sum specified in these rules shall be allowed to his wife, (if any) on her producing the certificate of her marriage, or other good proofs to the satisfaction of the society, or the person nomineed by him to receive the same, which nominee may be named on the member first joining the society, subject to any future alteration, and must be a relation or person having the charge of his funeral.

XXII. That if any member be forced into his majesty's service, and shall afterwards be discharged in good health and sound in his limbs, he may be re-admitted into the society, provided he pay up his arrears due at the time of his being impressed ; the same to extend to all members having already left the united kingdom ; but any person leaving after the 6th day of August, 1832, and shall remain abroad beyond the space of three years, shall be erased from the society, and forfeit all monies paid by him into the society's fund.

XXIII. Any member who may be induced to serve the office of headborough or constable, as a substitute, receiving a hurt or wound in the execution of the duties of such office, shall not be allowed any benefit from the funds, such hurt having been occasioned by a voluntary act of his own, except in case of death, when the usual sum shall be allowed, as specified in rule twenty-one ; but should any member be lawfully called upon to serve either of the aforesaid offices, and be hurt in performing the duties thereof, he shall be entitled to the same benefits as other members.

XXIV. That a box be provided with three locks and three keys, to be different from each other ; the first committee-man and president to have one each, the landlord the other ; and whoever neglects to bring his key in due time, shall be fined one shilling ; and if any one is absent and does not send his key the whole of the evening, he shall be fined two shillings and sixpence ; any member losing his key he shall provide another at his own expense. The landlord shall for the time being be the treasurer of the society, and shall give security, pursuant to 10 Geo. 4, c. 65, s. 11, and shall deliver the box, with its contents, whenever called upon by the committee ; and in the said box shall be deposited the cash, notes, rules, and other valuables belonging to the society. The box shall never be opened on any occasion excepting on the regular meeting nights, under the fine of ten shillings to each person holding the keys. The landlord shall provide candles, and a good fire when wanting, or be fined two shillings.

XXV. That this society be not dissolved, nor the

stock thereof shared, without the consent of five sixths of the then existing members, and agreeable to the statute 10 Geo. 4, c. 56, s. 26.

XXVI That on the quarterly night, which shall happen in July of each year, the members then assembled shall appoint three auditors, who, with the secretary, shall meet on the most convenient day before the following meeting night, to audit all the accounts and examine the books of the society for the past year, and report to the society the following meeting night, at which time the secretary shall cause to be delivered to the members a printed general statement of the funds and effects of or belonging to the society, specifying in whose custody or possession the said funds shall be then remaining, together with an account of all and various sums of money received and expended on account of the society, the said statement to be attested by the auditors and countersigned by the secretary ; the auditors and secretary to be allowed two shillings and sixpence each for their trouble ; and should either of them neglect to attend half an hour beyond the time of meeting, he shall be fined two shillings and sixpence; if an hour, he shall be fined five shillings, sickness excepted, of which due notice shall be given to the secretary, attested by a medical certificate ; the members to pay twopence each for the statement.

XXVII. Any member, previous to his becoming free, receiving an injury which may prevent him working in future, verified by a skilful medical man, and according with the opinions of a majority of the members present, the president shall direct the committee to adjudge the unfortunate member any sum not exceeding eight pounds, as the nature of the case may require, and he shall then be excluded.

XXVIII. When this society shall have money sufficient to purchase stock, they shall appoint three trustees at a meeting of at least one third of the society to transact business; and in case any one of the trustees shall embezzle or withhold any of the society's money, he or they shall be excluded from the society, and be prosecuted according to law. The interest to be placed in the hands of the president on the meeting nights in February and August, and if not paid accordingly, the person so offending shall be fined five shillings. The trustees to be chosen by ballot, and continue in office during the pleasure of the society, and the funds shall be invested pursuant to 10 Geo. 4, c. 56, s. 13-31, with the consent of the committee.

XXIX. That at a free member's death every member shall subscribe two shillings, and at a free member's wife's, one shilling.

XXX. That should the stock of this society be reduced to £400. sterling, each member shall subscribe three shillings per month in lieu of two shillings and fivepence, named in rule one, and when the stock shall be accumulated to £700. the subscriptions to be reduced to the regular sum.

XXXI. That all money arising from contributions and fines shall be applied to the purposes in these rules mentioned, and in defraying the necessary expenses attending the management of the affairs of the society; any officer misapplying the funds shall repay the same and be excluded.

XXXII. That these rules shall be considered binding on every member, and that no alteration shall take place but in conformity with 10 Geo. 4, c. 56 s. 9, at a general meeting convened for that purpose. Each member shall be supplied with a copy of these rules for which he shall pay sixpence.

FINIS.

CONTENTS.

I hereby certify that the foregoing rules, as corrected by me, are in conformity to law, and with the provisions of the Act 10 Geo. 4, c. 56, intituled " An Act to consolidate and amend the Laws relating to Friendly Societies".

(Signed) JOHN TIDD PRATT,

The Barrister at Law, appointed to certify the Rules of Saving's Banks.

4, *Elm Court, Temple,* 21*st May,* 1832.

FORM OF RETURN,

To be annexed to Rules, pursuant to 10 Geo. iv. c. 56, s. 34.

List of the Members of the UNITED PHILANTHROPISTS' SOCIETY, held at the *Half Moon, Strutton Ground*; established on the *11th August*, 1811, with a return of the Sickness and Mortality experienced therein for the period of Five Years, commencing January 1st, 18 , and ending December 31st, 18 .

NAMES. (N. B. This Column may be filled up with Initials.)	Trade or profession.	Date of Birth.	Date of Admission, into the Society.	Date of becoming a Free Member.	For what time entitled to Relief on account of Sickness.										For what time entitled to Relief on account of Superannuation.										Date of Death.	Place of Residence at time of death.	REMARKS.
					Weeks.	In 18	Weeks.	In 18	Weeks.	In 18	Weeks.	In 18	Weeks.	In 18	Weeks.	In 18	Weeks.	In 18	Weeks.	In 18	Weeks.	In 18	Weeks.	In 18			
					Days.		Days.		Days.		Days.		Days.		Days.		Days.		Days.		Days.		Days.				

I hereby certify that the transcribed Rules, of which the within is a Duplicate Copy, were allowed and confirmed by the Justices, present at the General Quarter Sessions of the Peace, held in and for the County of Middlesex, on Monday the first day of July, 1833, and that such transcript has been filed by me with the Rolls of the said Session of the Peace; dated the 1st day of July, 1833.

H. C. SELBY,

Clerk of the Peace.

RULES

OF THE

FRIENDLY SOCIETY

HELD AT

THE ANGEL INN, BEDFORD.

Established May the 29th, 1826.

BEDFORD:

HILL AND SON, PRINTERS, PAPERHANGERS, AND MACHINE-
RULERS, OLD MARKET PLACE.

1839,

To the Secretary of the Friendly Society held at the Angel Inn, Bedford.

I,   born in the Parish
of   in the County of   on
the   Day of   in the Year 18   ,
by Trade a   , being desirous of becoming
a Member of the above Society, Do HEREBY DECLARE and
set forth that I am not afflicted with any Disorder or
Constitutional Weakness which may tend to shorten life,
or to incapacitate me for the performance of my customary
occupation. And I do hereby agree that this Declaration
shall be the basis of the Contract between the Society and
myself, and that if any untrue averment is contained in this
Declaration, all monies which shall have been paid to the
Society on account thereof shall be forfeited : and I do
hereby consent to the Rules and Regulations of the said
Society.

Dated this   Day of   in the Year 18

(SIGNED)

Witness

RULES, &c.

ARTICLE I.

THAT this society is instituted for the purpose of relieving its members in cases of sickness, accidents, and bodily infirmities; and in cases of deaths, whether of members or members' wives, to defray the expenses of their interment; and shall hold their meetings at The ANGEL INN, St. Mary's, Bedford.

II.

The institution shall be under the management of two Trustees and two Directors (who shall be resident members) the secretary, and four stewards for the time being; who shall have full power to invest their funds, pursuant to the Act of George the fourth, c. 56, s. 13. The trustees shall be elected at a general meeting of the society, and continue in office during the pleasure of the society.

III.

That every person wishing to become a member of this society must signify the same to the secretary one month before he can be proposed for the society's approval ; and the meeting at which he shall be proposed he shall personally appear, with a certificate of his age and health if required : no person shall be admitted under the age of twenty nor above the age of thirty-five years. He must be a tradesman in the receipt of fifteen shillings per week, in sound health. free from hereditary disease or weakness, and of good moral character.

IV.

Every member shall pay or cause to be paid four shillings and sixpence per quarter to the stock, and sixpence per quarter to the auxiliary fund. No member can receive benefit from the society until he has been a member twelve months : members must clear the books every quarterly meeting, or be fined one shilling ; and if not paid to the secretary within one month after, he shall receive no benefit till the following quarter night ; then if not paid he shall be excluded. Quarterly payments are as follows :—

The first Monday in April,   from 7 to 9 in the evening.
The first Monday in July,   from 7 to 9 in the evening.
The first Monday in October, from 7 to 9 in the evening.
The 26th Day of December, from 10 to 1 in the forenoon.

V.

Any member claiming relief from the
funds of this society must produce a certificate from his medical attendant, stating
the nature of his disease; and if not within
four miles of Bedford, his certificate must
also be signed by the minister and churchwardens of the parish in which he resides,
and renewed every fourteen days; and any
expense that may occur to be paid by such
sick member. The stewards shall then in
such case, pay or cause to be paid the sum
of two shillings per day, Sundays excepted,
so long as he shall be sick or lame; providing such sickness or lameness does not continue more than six months. Should such
sickness or infirmity continue, then he shall
receive one shilling and fourpence per day
for the following six months: after such
time he shall receive not less than four shillings per week for the term of his natural
life, unless he recovers. If any member
shall have received twelve shillings or eight
shillings per week for a less period than
twenty-six weeks, he shall not be allowed
to begin his twenty-six on again on the re-
newal of sickness, until he shall have ceased
to receive any pay whatever on account of
sickness for twelve calendar months, but if
he fall ill within that time he shall be placed
in the same situation as when he ceased to

receive any relief, and shall receive such
relief and no other as he would have received
had no cessation of his sickness occurred.

VI.

That when any free member of this society shall die, his widow, or executor, or
person having charge of his funeral, shall
be entitled to the sum of six pounds, to be
paid by the stewards within two days after
his decease : but for want of heirs of credit
and respectability, the stewards are empowered to bury him decently, and not to
expend more than four pounds, and to provide a tomb-stone with a suitable inscription
which shall not cost more than two pounds.
On such occasions each member shall pay
or cause to be paid the sum of one shilling
at the next quarterly meeting after the decease of such member, and in default thereof shall pay a fine of two shillings and sixpence or be excluded. Every free member
at the death of his wife shall receive the
sum of four pounds within two days after
her decease. Members payment and fine
as above.

VII.

That one member of this society be chosen
secretary. Such secretary shall take care
of the books and keep all the accounts fairly ; he shall register all fines and monies

received and paid, and all certificates required by the rules of this society; he shall always attend the meetings at the appointed time or be fined one shilling, if absent half an hour one shilling and sixpence, and if entirely absent (except on the box) he shall provide a substitute, and also be fined two shillings and sixpence: and for attending to the duties of his office he shall receive for each member the sum of sixpence per annum.

VIII.

The stewards and members of this society shall be addressed by their proper names under a fine of twopence. The stewards are to keep silence and preserve the good order of the meetings; when they demand silence each member not obeying shall be fined twopence. The stewards neglecting their duty shall be fined sixpence; they shall always attend the meetings within a quarter of an hour of the appointed time or be fined sixpence, if absent altogether one shilling; they must always visit the sick twice a week alternately or pay a fine of one shilling for so neglecting. Every member detected in swearing, or using obscene talk or provoking language during club-hours, shall be fined for every offence threepence: every member breaking the peace and good order of the meeting by quarrelling, shall be fined two shillings; and if any member come disguised in liquor and refuse to leave the room when ordered by the stewards he shall be fined one shilling.

IX.

A yearly feast of this society shall be held on the twenty sixth day of December in every year, and every member must pay or cause to be paid one shilling and sixpence to defray the expenses of the same, or be fined one shilling and sixpence : no part of the expenses to come out of the funds of this society.

X.

That a surgeon be chosen annually by a majority of the members of this society, who shall receive such salary as the society may from time to time think proper to allow. The surgeon shall not be obliged to attend any member not residing within four miles of Bedford.

XI.

If any member is known to do any kind of work, or found drinking, or transacting any kind of business at a public-house, or in any way whatever imposing upon the society while receiving relief, upon proof thereof he shall be immediately expelled the society ; but he shall be allowed to give orders or write a receipt at his residence.

XII.

That no member shall receive benefit from the society's funds in such cases of sickness or infirmity, as shall be proved to the satisfaction of the society to have arisen from drunkenness, fighting, unlawful or needless exercise, or from immoral conduct of any kind.

XIII.

That the sum of one shilling and nine pence per head per annum be allowed for rent of club-room, and other incidental expenses.

XIV.

That if any member be convicted of felony, perjury, fraud, or notable crime, that may bring disgrace on the society, he shall be excluded.

XV.

That if any member of this society go to sea, or enter into Her Majesty's service by sea or land, he shall be excluded.

XVI.

All monies arising from contributions and fines shall be applied to the purposes in

these rules mentioned, and in defraying
the necessary expenses attending the management of the affairs of the society : any
officer misapplying the funds shall repay
the same and be excluded.

XVII.

That in case of dispute between this society and any member, or person claiming
on account of a member, reference shall be
made to arbitration, pursuant to 10 Geo. 4,
c. 56, s. 27. At the first meeting of the
society after the enrolment of these rules,
five arbitrators shall be named and elected,
none of them being directly or indirectly
beneficially interested in the funds of the
society ; and in each case of dispute the
names of the arbitrators shall be written on
pieces of paper and placed in a box or glass,
and the three whose names are first drawn
out by the complaining party, or by some
one on his or her behalf, shall be the arbitrators to decide the matter in dispute.

XVIII.

Members refusing to serve the office of
steward shall be under the fine of two shillings and sixpence.

XIX.

This society shall not be dissolved unless

with the consent of five-sixths of its members and agreeable to 10 Geo. 4, c. 56, s. 26.

XX.

The stewards shall once in every year cause to be prepared, pursuant to 10 Geo. 4, &c., a general statement of the funds and effects of this society, specifying in whose custody or possession the said funds and effects shall be then remaining, together with an account of all and every the various sums of money received and expended by or on account of the said society, since the publication of the preceding periodical statement; and every member shall be entitled to a copy thereof on the payment of twopence.

WILLIAM SMITH,⎫
JA$^{s.}$ FRANCIS, - - - ⎬ *Members.*
THO$^{s.}$ LUNT, - - -⎭

GEO. FRANCIS, *Secretary.*

London, November 26th, 1839.

I hereby certify that the foregoing Rules are in conformity to Law, and with the provisions of the Act 10 *Geo. IV., c.* 56, *as amended by* 4 *and* 5 *Wm. IV., c.* 40.

JOHN TIDD PRATT,

The Barrister at Law appointed to certify Rules of Savings Banks.

FINES.

FORMS

FOR DECLARING ON AND OFF THE BOX.

A Declaration shall be written and signed in the following terms, namely :—

I,   give notice this   Day
of   one thousand eight hundred and
that I am unable to work, being afflicted with
and therefore desire the Benefit of our Society.

(SIGNED)

Surgeon.

I,   give notice this   Day
of   one thousand eight hundred and
that I am, through the blessing of God, restored to health,
and am able to work; therefore declare that I shall no
longer want the Benefit of our Society, and that I have
received

(SIGNED)

FORM OF RETURN TO BE ANNEXED TO RULES,

Pursuant to 10 Geo. 4, c. 56, s. 34, and 4 & 5 Wm. 4, c. 40, s. 6.

LIST of the MEMBERS of the   Society, held at   established on the   Day of 18 , with a Return of the Sickness and Mortality experienced therein for the period of Five Years, commencing January 1, 18 , and ending December 31, 18

NAMES. [N.B.—*This Column may be filled up with Initials.*]	Trade or Profession.	Date of Birth.	Date of Admission into the Society.	Date of becoming a Free Member.	For what time entitled to Relief on account of Sickness.		For what time entitled to Relief on account of Superannuation		Date of Death.	Place of Residence at Time of Death.	REMARKS.
					weeks. days.	IN 18					
					weeks. days.	IN 18					
					weeks days	IN 18					
					weeks weeks. days.	IN 18					
					weeks. days.	IN 18					
					weeks days.	IN 18					
					weeks. days.	IN 18					
					weeks. days.	IN 18					
					weeks. days.	IN 18					
					weeks. days.	IN 18					

HILL AND SON,
PRINTERS, SILVER-STREET,
BEDFORD.

British Labour Struggles:
Contemporary Pamphlets 1727-1850

An Arno Press/New York Times Collection

The Factory Act of 1833. 1833-1834.

Richard Oastler: King of Factory Children. 1835-1861.

The Battle for the Ten Hours Day Continues. 1837-1843.

The Factory Education Bill of 1843. 1843.

Prelude to Victory of the Ten Hours Movement. 1844.

Sunday Work. 1794-1856.

Demands for Early Closing Hours. 1843.

Conditions of Work and Living: The Reawakening of the English Conscience. 1838-1844.

Improving the Lot of the Chimney Sweeps. 1785-1840.

The Rising of the Agricultural Labourers. 1830-1831.

The Aftermath of the "Lost Labourers' Revolt". 1830-1831.